ional Ethics

editors: Andrew Belsey and Ruth Chadwick
r Applied Ethics, University of Wales College

alism is a subject of interest to academics, the general public -be professional groups. Traditional ideas of professions and al conduct have been challenged by recent social, political ological changes. One result has been the development for ry profession of an ethical code of conduct which attempts se its values and standards. These codes of conduct raise of questions about the status of a 'profession' and the moral implications for behaviour.

ies, edited from the Centre for Applied Ethics in Cardiff, xamine these questions both critically and constructively. volumes will consider issues relevant to particular pro- ncluding nursing, genetics counselling and law. Other ill address issues relevant to all professional groups such ction and value of a code of ethics and the demands of lity.

ble in this series:

ues in Nursing
eoffrey Hunt

ues in Social Work
ichard Hugman and David Smith

unselling
ngus Clarke

d of Professional Ethics
n

Ethical Issues in Journ and the Media

All over the world codes of con journalists. In fact ethics is inseparat practice of journalism is centred concepts: freedom, democracy, trut If the proper role of journalism is then the ethical questions focus on o of the information.

This issue has become a matter of concern. Many people think the m The Robert Maxwell case has reop ship. Questions of censorship and arisen in connection with *Spycatch* Northern Ireland and the wars i Parliament has threatened statutory ship of the Press Complaints Comm cannot curb gross invasions of priv tabloid press. There is much co exploitative representation of wom

This book addresses issues suc philosophical and practical, critica topical. Accessible in approach, journalism, media studies and app appeal to the general reader.

Profes

Genera
Centre
of Card

Professio and wou professio and tech almost e to forma a numbe conseque

This se seeks to Individua fessions, volumes as the fu confidenti

Also avail

Ethical Is
Edited by

Ethical Is
Edited by

Genetic C
Edited by

The Grou
Daryl Koe

Ethical Issues in Journalism and the Media

Edited by
Andrew Belsey and Ruth Chadwick

Routledge
Taylor & Francis Group
LONDON AND NEW YORK

First published 1992
by Routledge
2 Park Square, Milton Park, Abingdon, Oxfordshire OX14 4RN

Simultaneously published in the USA and Canada
by Routledge
711 Third Avenue, New York, NY 10017

Routledge is an imprint of the Taylor and Francis Group, an informa business

First issued in hardback 2015

Reprinted 1995, 1998

Transferred to Digital Printing 2006

Typeset in 10 on 12 point Times by
Ponting–Green Publishing Services, Chesham, Bucks

British Library Cataloguing in Publication Data
A catalogue record for this book is available from the British Library

Library of Congress Cataloging in Publication Data
A catalog record for this book is available from the Library of Congress

ISBN 978-0-415-06927-4 (pbk)
ISBN 978-1-138-13194-1 (hbk)

Publisher's Note
The publisher has gone to great lengths to ensure the quality of this reprint but points out that some imperfections in the original may be apparent

Contents

Notes on contributors

Andrew Belsey is a lecturer in Philosophy and Honorary Secretary of the Centre for Applied Ethics, University of Wales College of Cardiff. His published articles, which have appeared in a variety of philosophical journals and books, include studies of ethical and political issues in science, medicine, technology and literature.

David Burnet is a lecturer in the Cardiff Law School, University of Wales College of Cardiff. Apart from media law, his interests include legal philosophy and housing law.

Ruth Chadwick is a lecturer in Philosophy and Director of the Centre for Applied Ethics, University of Wales College of Cardiff. She is the editor of *Ethics, Reproduction and Genetic Control* (London, Routledge, 1990) and joint author, with Win Tadd, of *Ethics and Nursing Practice: A Case Study Approach* (Basingstoke, Macmillan, 1992).

Andrew Edgar studied Sociology at Lancaster University, and then did research at Sussex University on aesthetics and the sociology of culture in the context of post-Kantian German philosophy. He has taught ethics and social theory at Newcastle-upon-Tyne Polytechnic, and is now a lecturer in Philosophy, University of Wales College of Cardiff, where he is a member of both the Centre for Applied Ethics and the Centre for Critical and Cultural Theory.

Paul Gilbert is currently Head of the Department of Philosophy at the University of Hull. His main research interests lie in applied philosophy and the philosophy of mind. He has published several papers on terrorism and the violence of the State. He is the author of *Human Relationships: A Philosophical Introduction* (Oxford, Blackwell, 1991).

Bruce Hanlin holds degrees in Media Studies, Film Studies and American Studies, and has been teaching in these areas since 1982. He has worked at the polytechnics in Coventry, Newcastle-upon-Tyne and North London, and currently teaches courses in media theories and organisations in the Graduate Centre for Journalism, City University, London, and in film and television at the Centre for Extra-Mural Studies, Birkbeck College, University of London.

Nigel G.E. Harris is a senior lecturer in Philosophy at the University of Dundee. His main interests are in applied ethics, especially business and professional ethics, and in seventeenth- and eighteenth-century ethics and epistemology. He is the author of *Professional Codes of Conduct in the United Kingdom: A Directory* (London, Mansell, 1989), and is currently working on a bibliographical guide to works in media ethics.

Jennifer Jackson is a lecturer in Philosophy and Director of the Centre for Business and Professional Ethics at the University of Leeds. She has published articles on toleration, on euthanasia, and on honesty in marketing and medical practice.

John O'Neill is a lecturer in Philosophy at the University of Sussex, having previously taught at University College, Bangor, Lancaster University, and in Beijing. In addition to papers in many philosophical journals, his publications include *Worlds Without Content: Against Formalism* (London, Routledge, 1991). A play of his has been broadcast on BBC Radio 3.

Teresa Stratford is an occupational therapist who is currently Deputy Chair of the Campaign for Press and Broadcasting Freedom. She has taught WEA classes on issues related to media freedom, and has written on the subject for the Women's Press and Prism Press.

Kevin Williams is a lecturer in Media Studies at the Centre for Journalism Studies, University of Wales College of Cardiff. He has written numerous books and articles on war reporting, including, with Derrik Mercer and Geoff Mungham, *The Fog of War: The Media on the Battlefield* (London, Heinemann, 1987), and he is a co-author of the Glasgow University Media Group's *War and Peace News* (Milton Keynes, Open University Press, 1985).

General editors' foreword

Applied Ethics is now acknowledged as a field of study in its own right. Much of its recent development has resulted from rethinking traditional medical ethics in the light of new moral problems arising out of advances in medical science and technology. Applied philosophers, ethicists and lawyers have devoted considerable energy to exploring the dilemmas emerging from modern medical practice and its effects on the doctor–patient relationship.

But the point can be generalised. Even in health care, ethical dilemmas are not confined to medical practitioners but also arise in the practice of, for example, nursing. Beyond health care, other groups are beginning to think critically about the kind of service they offer and about the nature of the relationship between provider and recipient. In many areas of life social, political and technological changes have challenged traditional ideas of practice.

One visible sign of these developments has been the proliferation of codes of ethics, or of professional conduct. The drafting of such a code provides an opportunity for professionals to examine the nature and goals of their work, and offers information to others about what can be expected from them. If a code has a disciplinary function, it may even offer protection to members of the public.

But is the existence of such a code itself a criterion of a profession? What exactly is a profession? Can a group acquire professional status, and if so, how? Does the label 'professional' have implications, from a moral point of view, for acceptable behaviour, and if so how far do they extend?

This series, edited from the Centre for Applied Ethics in Cardiff, seeks to examine these questions both critically and constructively. Individual volumes will address issues relevant to all professional groups, such as the nature of a profession, the function and value of codes of ethics, and the demands of confidentiality. Other volumes will examine issues relevant to particular professions, including those which have hitherto received little attention, such as journalism, law and genetics counselling.

Andrew Belsey
Ruth Chadwick

Preface

The practice of journalism as a profession raises many ethical issues. We are more concerned with the nature and possible resolution of the issues that arise in the practice than with the theoretical definition of a profession. The nature of professionalism is both vague and flexible, as older professions like law and medicine change, and newer occupations jostle for the status that professionalism brings, occupations like teaching, social work, nursing, and even journalism. One thing that unites all claimants to the status, however, is an explicit concern for ethical standards in the conduct of the professionals. Cynics will say that ethics and journalism are incompatible, but this misses the real point. It might be that journalists, or indeed members of any professional group, do not always meet the expected standard in their conduct, but what this fact demonstrates is the relevance, not the irrelevance, of ethics to the profession.

This is certainly true of journalism. Much of the practice of journalism must be described and analysed in terms of a set of concepts which are essentially ethical, terms like freedom, objectivity, truth, honesty, privacy. Even democracy, the context in which so much discussion of the media takes place, is really an ethical term, since it is concerned with the right or the best form of social and political organisation. Ethics, then, is inseparable from journalism, and ethical discussion must be a part of understanding journalism, its practice and its problems.

This is the spirit in which this book is offered to its readers. As a work of applied philosophy it is both critical, as any philosophical – including ethical – discussion must be, and constructive, while recognising that no finality can be claimed. While there might be a broad consensus on many issues, a number of viewpoints are represented in the book, by authors from a variety of backgrounds, including philosophy, law and media studies.

Our own opening survey focuses on the issue of quality. We look first at the requirement, in a world faced by major problems, for the free flow of information on a global scale, undistorted by either any kind of censorship or a bias imposed by monopolistic structures of ownership. We then ask whether in a national context like the United Kingdom media quality can be enhanced by law or ethics, and we examine some of the philosophical problems involved in the idea of a code of conduct.

The next three papers develop some of these themes in more detail. John O'Neill challenges the liberal orthodoxy that the free market, journalism and democracy form an interdependent trinity. Claiming that the value of truth-telling is constitutive of journalism as a democratic institution, O'Neill argues that in fact the market inhibits the realising of this value. Bruce Hanlin examines the ownership structures of the British press and the effects of proprietorship on the practice of journalism. He concentrates on the sad saga of Robert Maxwell, a story that because of Britain's restrictive libel laws could not be told until after Maxwell's death in November 1991, and at the time of writing is still a long way from being told in full. David Burnet then looks at the formidable range of legal restrictions on the British media, and points out that the judiciary continues to be more favourably disposed towards excessive official secrecy than towards freedom of expression. He argues that recent changes to secrecy and security legislation do not have the liberalising character officially claimed for them.

Nigel G.E. Harris looks at the idea of a code of conduct for journalists, and raises questions including the nature, content and purposes of such a code. The next four papers take up issues with which a code of conduct is – or certainly should be – concerned. Andrew Belsey, while supporting a right to privacy, argues that its application is perhaps more restricted than is often thought, because of the nature of public life and the imperfections of democracy. Jennifer Jackson asks whether there are limits to honesty in investigative journalism, and suggests the working out, on the model of medical ethics, of more substantial principles of conduct in journalism. Andrew Edgar argues on the basis of a hermeneutic approach that objectivity in journalism cannot consist of achieving the truth in the sense of correspondence with the facts but rather of the avoidance of bias. Teresa Stratford then criticises the sexist and stereotyped presentation and treatment of women, especially in Britain's tabloid newspapers, and suggests that the press should catch up with public opinion in recognising the changed role and status of women in today's society.

The final two papers are concerned with the reporting of terrorism and war. Paul Gilbert queries the arguments that might be used to support the broadcasting ban on alleged terrorists and their supporters introduced by the British Government in 1988. Kevin Williams then looks at censorship and self-censorship in war reporting. He discusses several reasons why journalists impose restrictions upon themselves: to protect the security of the forces at the front; to maintain morale among troops and civilians; and to protect the sensitivities of the home audience, which might not want to receive disturbing reports and images.

Although the contents of this book range widely, they by no means exhaust the topics that could be discussed under the heading of ethical issues in journalism and the media. There is still much more to say about freedom of expression and censorship in general, together with practical proposals for achieving more democratic structures within the media themselves, so that they can better serve the ends of democracy on a global scale, which should be their central concern. Other particular topics which could be examined in more detail include the right of reply, confidentiality, cheque-book journalism, homophobia, racism, and the appallingly ignorant and sensationalist treatment of AIDS.

What this shows is, we believe, that the scope for further philosophical and ethical reflection on journalism and media issues is considerable. Perhaps a second volume is called for? But meanwhile we hope that this present volume will make some contribution towards the ethical examination of professional practice in journalism and the media.

We should like to thank the contributors for the speedy and efficient way in which they responded to our invitation to take part in this project, and for their calmness when faced with subsequent editorial demands.

Andrew Belsey and Ruth Chadwick

Cardiff, 27 January 1992

Chapter 1

Ethics and politics of the media: the quest for quality

Andrew Belsey and Ruth Chadwick

Journalism is an honourable profession, though many of those who should care for it, often including its own professionals, have dishonoured it. Governments of most ideological leanings, when not actively persecuting it, have sought to censor and control it, usually with success. Owners have used it as a means of satisfying their quest for power and wealth, not to mention megalomania. As for journalists, they, as the humorous rhyme reminds us, do not even need to be bribed to behave unethically. Even 'consumers' have done journalism no service by putting up with trivia and trash, accepting execrable standards as the norm.

Yet journalism remains an honourable profession, because it has an honourable aim, the circulation of information, including news, comment and opinion. This is an honourable aim because the health of a community – especially a community that has any pretensions to democracy – depends on it. There is no reason why journalism should not have further aims as well, such as entertainment, so long as these are subordinated to the overall aim of the circulation of information.

Many of the issues raised so far are taken up in the essays in this book, and some of them will be commented on later in this introduction. But we are also concerned with the question of whether the honour of journalism can be restored, and with the global context which matters to do with community, democracy and the media cannot ignore as the world approaches the millennium. In both cases the issue of *quality* will be at the forefront.

THE GLOBAL CONTEXT

Unprecedented changes as the world enters the final decade of the twentieth century present the media with great opportunities and great problems. The opportunities arise from the global need for information as human beings assess the chances of their own survival as a species, or, at a less fateful level, just worry about what sort of world and what sort of life for its inhabitants there will be in the future. Global politics presents daunting challenges, but authoritarian structures are no longer regarded as an acceptable means to political ends. The sort of alternative democratic participation and involvement that is required is impossible without information. Here then, as the people of the world struggle for a worthwhile way of life within a sustainable future, is a role for the media, especially those media that can still be called the press, whether they are part of print or broadcast journalism, so long as they follow the traditional role of the press as providers of information.

It is something of a cliché that the world has shrunk to a village in which the major problems are problems for everyone, for they are unavoidable and cannot be escaped from by futile attempts to keep your own back yard clean. Further, it is said that the world has become an electronic village, for almost everyone has instant access through radio and television and newer electronic media to the latest circulated information. But it is precisely the quality of this information which is at issue.

The major problems facing humanity seem to arise from an unstable mixture of politics and science, using both these terms in a broad sense. First of all there is the global problem of environment, resources and population, a single whole which is a compound of numerous elements. These include the problem of feeding the world's hungry, which could be done now if existing food resources were distributed properly and fairly (though the effect on world food supply of the collapse of the Soviet Union remains to be assessed). But even so, there is an upward pressure on all resources as the world population continues to grow exponentially, and at the same time the environment faces increasing degradation from pollution of all kinds, including that which contributes to the alleged greenhouse effect.

In addition, national rivalries, often over resources, but fuelled by chauvinistic, ideological and religious differences, threaten to bring permanent instability to international relations, together with the constant threat of war based on the mass availability of sophisticated weaponry, including perhaps nuclear weapons released by the break-up of the Soviet Union. The falling-apart of this once fairly stable structure is itself a major world problem, promising a very uncertain future for the inhabitants of the former political conglomerate, together with highly unpredictable consequences for the rest of the world, as a large part of the largest continent faces the prospect of involuntary transfer from the Second World to the Third, unless some sort of stable and reasonably prosperous future can be invented for it.

Underlying the other problems is something which itself is a problem, science. It promises so much and yet threatens even more. Instead of being the disinterested pursuit of knowledge allied to the application of theoretical advances to worthwhile practical projects of global significance, science has become a commodity, dedicated to the production of further commodities for the market, from nuclear power stations to microscopic eavesdropping devices to artificially engineered viruses. Taken over by capitalism, science has become the slave of a consumerism which demands the instant gratification of the latest want, whether it be for a piece of electronic wizardry or a genetically perfect baby.

The dissemination and discussion of information concerning the major problems the world and its people face is necessary to both the democratic understanding and the democratic action without which the problems cannot be solved – without which, in fact, they will escalate. So here is a great opportunity for the media to contribute to the advancement of peace, prosperity and progress. But can the media respond effectively? For they themselves are not free from many of the problems that contribute to the world's difficulties.

It is another cliché that the question of the relations of production has been replaced by the question of the relations of information and communication; but as is the case with many political clichés there is a good deal of ideological fog about this one. With one fifth of the world's population – one billion people – in a state of dire physical need, questions about the production, distribution and consumption, the ownership and control, of the world's material resources will continue to be of central relevance and importance to the political agenda.

No doubt questions about information and communication have increased in significance and will continue to do so, but they are the same questions, about production, distribution and consumption, ownership and control. Furthermore, it would be a mistake to regard the world's informational and communicational resources as any less material than its food and mineral resources.

All the different questions about information can be brought into focus on the issue of *quality*. In the light of the problems the world faces, the typical daily content of an American television channel or a British tabloid newspaper is not just a shame but a crime. This is at a time when many parts of the world with no tradition of a free press are trying to develop media that better serve and reflect the rising tide of democracy, and are looking to the West for models to emulate. But disappointment and disillusionment could quickly follow. For in addition to stunning triviality, these searchers after new exemplars will find enormous concentration of ownership in the hands of transnational corporations, together with governments who think little of selling television channels to the highest bidder.

However, governments with a purely 'market' approach to communications are not the only ones with no interest in the free flow of information. This, however, raises the interesting question of whether it is now possible for individual governments to have much control over the information available to their populations. The Islamic Salvation Front, which won the first round of the Algerian election late in 1991, proposed (in addition to the suppression of the civil and political rights of women) to 'challenge the vibrant independent press'.[1] But could they have done it? No doubt newspapers can be closed down and journalists persecuted, but even the former Soviet bloc, with its strict controls on printing presses, photocopiers, duplicators and even typewriters, was unable to suppress the underground press. But this was old technology, and new authoritarian rulers cannot achieve their aims without a major and unprecedented act of techno-censorship which would ban faxes, computer networks and satellite dishes.[2]

For many years the apartheid regime in South Africa held out against a television network on the grounds that it would corrupt the moral fibre of the people – meaning, of course, challenge the survival of the potentially unstable minority regime. When the government finally gave in over television, many people predicted the end of apartheid. They were correct, although whether there has been any causal connection is much harder to establish.

But any investigation of this would have to make some sort of stab at distinguishing between form and content, a distinction often attacked these days, but one which is unavoidable when considering global informational flow. For some forms of media can be more convivial than others, to use Illich's term.[3] Desktop publishing and local electronic networks, for instance, can be organised in co-operative and participatory structures which encourage communitarian and democratic outlooks and behaviour. Global, monopolistic media networks controlled by transnational corporations are more likely to pander to a passive consumerism with negative psychological and political consequences. There is nothing inevitable about these outcomes, of course. Local networks might encourage parochialism and hostile nationalisms, while global networks might promote cosmopolitanism and internationalism, as telephones and fax machines already have. But whatever form the informational structures take, there is still the matter of their content, and more especially, its quality.

Still, on the global level the need for information to enable people to play their parts as citizens of the world is indisputable, and the opportunities for the media are therefore legion. But beyond this, because both the politics and the technology of the media are rapidly changing in unpredictable ways, it is questions rather than answers that suggest themselves as conclusions. Who will provide, produce, edit, control and distribute the information? If it is local networks, how can they provide the necessary international outlook? If it is global monopolies, how can they be encouraged to have aims more responsible than the mere pursuit of profit? Can the media play down national, ideological and other rivalries and emphasise common humanity facing common problems? As old totalitarianisms collapse, how can the threat from new ones be overcome without plunging the world into further risks of war?

These questions raise the issue of whether the pursuit of profit or power is compatible with quality in the media, and this in turn raises the question of freedom. What is meant by a 'free press'? Is it the freedom of democratically elected governments (no matter how imperfect the democracy) to propose and dispose? Is it the freedom of corporations or individual owners to buy up large chunks of the world's media and to mould them in their image? Is it the freedom of editors to decide what gets broadcast or published? Is it the freedom of journalists to offer fact and opinion without fear of sanction or persecution? Or is it the freedom of ordinary people to receive full and fair information on all issues that are likely to affect their lives and their interests?

QUALITY CONTROL: LAW OR ETHICS?

Turning now from the global to the national level, we find that the issue of quality is still inescapable. A free and vigorous press and other organs of mass media and mass communications are agreed to be among the essential ingredients of a healthy democracy. (We include the word 'vigorous' because it is clear that freedom is not sufficient: a press could be free yet timid or torpid.) This need for media freedom is recognised in various charters and conventions of human rights, as well as in, famously, the First Amendment to the Constitution of the United States of America. In Britain, however, the media are already more restricted by the law, both criminal and civil, than in most other countries of the democratic world. So can the law act as a mechanism for quality control, or should this be rather a matter of morality – of ethics? But is it really wise to suggest yet further restrictions of any sort, however inspiring the idea of moral principles and ethical codes of conduct might initially sound?

In Britain the media are restricted by the criminal laws of official secrets, obscenity, blasphemy, sedition, and reporting restrictions on Irish terrorist groups and their alleged supporters; by the civil laws of libel and breach of confidence; and by the judge-made law of contempt of court. In addition to the laws themselves there is the problem of a judiciary generally unsympathetic to the ideas of a free press and freedom of information and firmly wedded to prior restraint through the use of interlocutory ('gagging') injunctions, a legal move virtually impossible in the United States.

But there is nothing obscure about the difference between the British and American situations. It is a matter of the different constitutions, but beyond this, a fundamental cleavage in political ideology. Britain is not a republic of citizens but a monarchy of subjects, living in a system in which parliament is both supreme in legislation, largely independent of judicial review, and yet still hemmed in by crown prerogative exercised by the government of the day. Subjects do not, or indeed cannot, have rights in the way citizens can, which is why the British constitution finds it so hard to accommodate itself to the European Convention on Human Rights, or to incorporate it into domestic legislation. Nor can the constitution recognise freedom of information: British public life depends on a strictly interpreted need-to-know principle, and those who are on the receiving end of government – the electorate – are not regarded as needing to know. The fact that this fetters the exercise of the supposedly democratic franchise is a problem hardly yet tackled except by pressure groups like Liberty, Charter 88 and the Campaign for Freedom of Information, and the depth of the problem is shown by the further fact that individual members of parliament are little better off than their constituents when it comes to access to information.

The general laws of the land and the peculiarities of the constitution do not exhaust the legal controls over the British media. Broadcasting is subject to a number of statutory licensing and regulating bodies, including the Independent Television Commission, the Radio Authority, the Broadcasting Complaints Commission and the Broadcasting Standards Council. This system of controls has been criticised for several reasons, including the charge that the bodies have unclear and overlapping jurisdictions. The Broadcasting Complaints Commission, for instance, is supposed to deal with complaints concerning matters such as lack of factual accuracy, unfairness in presentation and intrusions into privacy, whereas the Broadcasting Standards Council deals with alleged offences against taste and decency in the areas of sex, violence, bad language and the treatment of disasters. But broadcasters have found the bodies to have expansionist ambitions, while at the same time being narrow-minded and generally unsympathetic to the claims of media freedom.[4]

In the case of print journalism there is no statutory regulatory body, but the peculiar history and status of the Press Complaints Commission (PCC) might suggest that there is no real difference. In 1990 the Report of the Calcutt Committee on Privacy and Related Matters proposed that the previous voluntary body, the Press Council, which had become widely regarded on all sides as ineffective, should be replaced by the new PCC, the function of which would be to supervise a code of practice drawn up by the newspaper industry itself.[5] The Calcutt Committee further proposed that this double-act would have 18 months, starting 1 January 1991, to clean up the industry, and more especially to eliminate intrusions into private lives, otherwise parliament should feel free to introduce statutory protection for privacy. (The Calcutt Committee had proposed that physical intrusion, including 'doorstepping' and electronic eavesdropping, should become illegal.) The press, rightly alarmed that neither the draconian nature of this intimidation nor the disastrous consequences of trying to enforce it would inhibit parliamentary action, has attempted what was probably intended all along: to behave better. At the time of writing the press is still undergoing its period of probation.[6]

So what have the actual and potential legislative and statutory barriers done for the quality of the British media? Very little, but this is hardly surprising, since the emphasis has been on restriction, on negativity, on what the media must not publish, rather than on the quality of what does appear on screens and pages. Only in one area – a reduction of the more vile or grotesque invasions of privacy by the tabloid press – has this negative approach had a beneficial effect. But if there has been at least this consequence, might it not be taken further, by giving privacy some statutory protection? The problem with this is that it would almost certainly have a severely deleterious effect on serious journalism, while leaving untouched the trivia and gossip that form the staple of the tabloids. And in general any legal restriction on the press, in the absence of a constitutional guarantee of press freedom and some sort of freedom of information legislation, is a one-sided detraction, preventing the press from fulfilling a proper democratic role.

So is it to ethics, and self-regulation along the lines of the PCC, that one should look for the protection and enhancement of quality? Clearly, even if (most) legal restrictions were lifted, ethics in journalism would still be required, and it is notable than in the USA, where the law is less restrictive, ethical debate among both theoreticians and practitioners of journalism is lively, widespread and accepted as normal. Ethical discussion is essential because there are many ways in which the media can offend without straying beyond the law: inaccuracy, lies, distortions, bias, propaganda, favouritism, sensationalism, trivialisation, lapses of taste, vulgarity, sleaze, sexism, racism, homophobia, personal attacks, smears, character assassination, cheque-book journalism, deception, betrayal of confidences and invasions of privacy. And this is by no means a complete list.

CODES AND ETHICS

Surveys show that the press (especially the tabloid press) is held in low esteem by the public for offending in many of the ways just listed,[7] and although this fact in itself tells us nothing about the ethical quality of the press, it does suggest that a start could be made on quality control by contemplating the introduction of a code of conduct which would prohibit these journalistic malpractices and provide that journalists be accountable for their actions.

The further possibility has been suggested, on the model of the medical and nursing professions, that journalists who violate the requirements of the professional code should be removed from a 'professional register', and thus prevented from practising. Against this it might be argued that the nature of the harm (for example, injury to health) which can arise out of a health-care professional's malpractice is much more serious than the harm (for example, invasion of privacy) that can be caused by that of a journalist. This could be questioned, however, for in some parts of the world, a journalist's indiscretion could put in danger the life of the subject of a news story. Also, if harms can be measured on a scale of distress, some cases of invasion of privacy may cause more distress than certain kinds of injury to health. Nevertheless, the idea that a journalist should be licensed to practise – with the licence being removed for serious violations of a code of conduct – is surely too draconian and anti-democratic a solution to the problem of media malpractice.

Whatever the disciplinary mechanism associated with a code, it is likely that a code of conduct will play an essential part in quality assurance. A number of supplementary issues arise, however, the first of which is what the content of the code should be, and whether it should be specified in broad-sweep principles or closely defined points of detail. But whichever approach is chosen, there will be the further issue which eternally crops up whenever applied moral issues are discussed: where do you draw the line? Several contributors to this book are concerned in different ways with this issue.

Take honesty. Yes, journalists should certainly be honest in their activities, in both investigating and reporting. But suppose some public corruption can be investigated only under cover, with the journalist pretending to be someone ready to make a corrupt deal? Or suppose there is a war on, and the journalist discovers something that might harm the war effort? Take privacy. A journalist might have the highest regard for the right to privacy, but claim that some information about a politician doesn't qualify for this protection. Or take the broadcasting ban on terrorism. Even if some aspects of the ban can be defended, is it fair or in the interests of democracy to extend it to archive material of genuine historical and political interest? Or is it reasonable to prevent the broadcasting of the actual speaking voice of an alleged terrorist supporter while allowing him or her to be shown on film with an actor reading synchronised words?[8] It is not difficult to think that wherever the line should be drawn it should not be drawn here. But the general problem remains, both in this and many other cases. Moreover, however much effort is put into drawing clear lines in a code of conduct, it is the individual journalist who will come face to face with very difficult ethical dilemmas, and have to make moral choices. No code can anticipate every situation.

Another issue arising from the idea of a code of conduct is whether it should be negative or positive, emphasising the avoidance of unethical conduct or the promotion of ethical conduct. Of course, these are almost the two sides of the same coin, but not quite, for 'Do not lie' is not equivalent to 'Tell the truth'. Lying, as everyone knows from daily-life situations, can be avoided by silence, vagueness or changing the subject, which suggests that not lying is an insufficient ethical principle, in both daily life and journalism. A newspaper might just keep quiet about facts which could produce embarrassment for a cause it supports. But then again as almost everyone realises, telling the truth is not without its problems too, for the truth is endless and seamless, whereas the exigencies of time and resources require some selection to be made from the potentially infinite. Of course, selection should be done in ways that are fair and balanced – but where do you draw the line?

The final issue to be raised here is that of the basis of an ethical code of conduct. Ethics is not (just) a matter of codes of conduct (plus or minus sanctions), not just a matter of rules to be followed. It is more to do with principles concerning the rights and wrongs of human conduct, principles which have some reasoned theoretical basis and which therefore apply objectively and impartially. Of course, this is not the same as saying that we know what these principles are: the search for them and their refinement will continue as long as human beings survive to debate and argue; but it is precisely the reasoned and democratic nature of this discussion that differentiates ethical principles from dogmatic pronouncements. To some extent ethical principles are, as Jonathan Glover has suggested, analogous to scientific theories:[9] they are not, and cannot be, handed down by an authority, but have to be discovered through the ingenious interplay of human reason and human experience, a process which while producing results of great value in both science and ethics is both fallible and endless.

In the interim, however, a code of conduct does require a reasoned basis in ethical theory, but the bonus of offering such a basis is that it can throw light on some of the other issues raised above, such as where to draw the line. Consider a code which is formulated in terms of rights. The mere assertion of rights might appear to have great political significance, but it lacks credibility and force unless a theoretical justification of rights claims can be offered. However, if such a justification is forthcoming, it might suggest a solution to the line-drawing problem. For example, if people have a right not to be deceived, then deception in investigative journalism, even for results which would be for the general benefit of the public, would not be permitted at all. But it is doubtful whether this solution is satisfactory, for presumably people also have a right not to be defrauded, so if the fraud can be exposed only through deception by journalists, which right should prevail? But if it is the fraudsters who are being deceived, do they have legitimate grounds for complaint? Perhaps these queries about rights-based theories cannot be answered by rights-based theories themselves.

So an alternative approach to seeking a reasoned basis for a code of conduct would be to look to some variation on a utilitarian theme, such as the theory that conduct should maximise the satisfaction of the interests of those to whom the conduct is directed, which in the case of journalism is presumably the general public or those members of it who are affected by the acquiring or publishing of a particular story. This would link the values of journalism to wider pre-existing community and political values like democracy, justice and the public good. But the idea of making the ethics of journalism subservient to these wider values, though plausible, brings out a difficulty in the notion of journalism as a profession. Traditionally a profession has been defined in terms of a relationship of trust between the individual practitioner and the individual client, law and medicine being the obvious examples. Here any public benefit would accrue as a by-product of the primary one-to-one relationship. Journalism clearly is not a profession in this sense, even though some parts of a code of conduct for journalists will inevitably be concerned with a journalist's duty to particular individuals, such as protecting the confidentiality of sources or respecting the privacy of people in the news. But the promotion of democracy, if that is to be regarded as part of the ethics of journalism, is not a duty owed to particular individuals. Nevertheless, a code ought to be not just compatible with, but in accordance with, wider moral and social values.

Yet a third approach to finding a reasoned basis for a code of conduct would be to anchor the conduct in a virtuous character, one that for journalists would exhibit specific virtues such as fairness, truthfulness, trustworthiness and non-malevolence.[10] Whereas this again has considerable plausibility, two comments are called for. First, if there are professional virtues they are not independent of whatever virtues there ought to be in general. But this is no criticism of this approach, as the whole object of providing a reasoned basis for a code of conduct is to link it with a general moral framework.

Second, however, it can be asked whether the general notion of virtue is actually foundational, because the virtuous character might well be explained further as precisely the one who respects the rights of others or who attempts to promote the general good.

Clearly, the matter of providing a reasoned basis in ethical theory for a code of conduct is neither simple nor something on which consensus is likely, and so this question, together with the other issues raised in this section, will continue to be debated. The important thing is to keep the discussion going.

QUALITY AND THE RESTORATION OF THE HONOUR OF JOURNALISM

We have already briefly commented on the question of whether journalism is a profession if it lacks the basic one-to-one practitioner–client relationship. The fact is, though, that this question is not particularly important. Even the traditional professions like law and medicine are no longer as rigid about this relationship as they used to be; and other professions like teaching or social work exhibit a variety of models of the practitioner–client relationship. What is important is not a precise definition of a profession, which is bound to be too restricted to apply to the variety of groups that have some fair claim to be professional these days, but rather the *quality* of the conduct of members of these groups, whether it be in medicine or journalism, so long as it has a potential for good or harm. What is important is that the activity that wishes to call itself professional be conducted on an ethical basis and that its practitioners be accountable for their actions.

So there is no reason why the concern of the original professions for an ethical basis – traditionally justified by the need to protect the interests of potentially vulnerable clients – should not be generalised to apply to the looser conception of a profession appropriate today. So professions should continue to be essentially concerned with standards of service, and to be value-guided, and typically to incorporate these concerns in an ethical code of conduct.

In journalism such a code can be regarded as involving two broad aspects, the input and the output. The latter is what is finally produced by the practice of journalism, the reports, articles and programmes, the information that actually reaches the public. Here it is plausible to suggest that the fundamental value is truth-telling, but as we have already suggested, this simple idea is complicated in practice, for the truth cannot be the whole truth. So principles of selection are required, which are themselves further values: fairness, justice, democratic significance and avoidance of bias and harm.

For the input of journalism, the day-to-day practice of journalists as they go about their profession, it is plausible to suggest that the fundamental value is honesty, but again the realisation of this value in practice is not simple, and other values will also have to be called upon.

Even if the fundamental values behind ethical conduct are regarded as somehow beyond dispute, this neither produces a code nor settles all questions about conduct. Partly because of the interplay of values within a code and partly because there is always scope for improvement as general ethical discussion continues, no code of conduct can be regarded as fixed and final. For if a code for journalists should be partially dedicated to the ends of democracy, the code itself is also subject to democratic means, to the sway of reasoned argument and discussion of the fundamentals of ethical and political life. Thus the question arises (as in the case of other professional groups) whether it is adequate for professionals to devise their own code without allowing for lay input into the drafting procedures.

The ultimate reason for having a code of conduct is to ensure quality, and so we return to the issue with which we opened, the restoration of the honour of journalism. We suggest that in both input and output it is the relentless pursuit of quality which can restore journalism's lost honour. But success in this pursuit faces enormous obstacles, especially in the area of output which, because of the essential democratic function of information, is probably the most serious barrier to the restoration of honour. In Britain at the present time the major obstacle is the lack of a legal or constitutional guarantee of freedom of information, as this lack directly contradicts values such as truth, justice, balance and democratic significance. But unfortunately the problem is not just governmental or legal barriers, but something deeper: a generally attenuated attachment to the importance of media freedom as a means to, and as part of, the attainment of a genuinely democratic and fair society. Information is power, and an extremely inegalitarian distribution of power is incompatible with professed democratic ideals. So what is required is a thorough commitment by government, political parties, the judiciary, business, the owners and controllers of the media, editors, journalists and the general public to freedom of information. Without it the idea of a charter for citizens is nonsensical.

What is true on a national level is also true internationally. A commitment to quality of information and information flow to meet the urgent and demanding need for action in a troubled world is required on a global scale. To ensure freedom of information on this scale both global networks and democratic access are essential. Here the enemies of freedom are perhaps even more formidable, though intolerant or totalitarian governments and transnational capitalist corporations are not natural allies, and to some extent their interests conflict. But whether censorship – ideological, religious or commercial – can prevail against the need for quality in the global media is not something that can today be predicted.

NOTES

1 Victoria Brittain, 'Islamic Victory Erases Algeria's Model Image', *Guardian*, 2 January 1992. The Front was denied final victory when the second round of voting was cancelled.
2 Even the regime in Saudi Arabia, which imposes one of the strictest censorships in the world, has been unable to deal with satellite television and the ubiquitous fax machine. See *Silent Kingdom: Freedom of Expression in Saudi Arabia* (London, Article 19, 1991), esp. pp. 18–19, 32.
3 Ivan Illich, *Tools for Conviviality* (London, Calder & Boyars, 1973).
4 Georgina Henry, 'A Mania for All Seasons', *Guardian*, 22 July 1991 (on the Broadcasting Standards Council); John Wilson, 'The Victims of a Galloping Lurgy', *Guardian*, 22 July 1991, and Ray Fitzwalter, 'Tales Wag the Watchdog', *Guardian*, 14 October 1991 (on the Broadcasting Complaints Commission).
5 Home Office, *Report of the Committee on Privacy and Related Matters* (Chairman, David Calcutt) (London, HMSO, 1990). On the PCC and the Code of Practice, see Press Complaints Commission, *Briefing* (London, PCC [1991]).
6 Maggie Brown, 'Newspapers Pass First Test of Self-Regulation', and Michael Leapman, 'Now Showing: Muckbusters II', *The Independent*, 18 September 1991.
7 Peter Kellner, 'Nobody Trusts Us and That's Bad News', *The Independent*, 7 August 1991.
8 See K.D. Ewing and C.A. Gearty, *Freedom Under Thatcher: Civil Liberties in Modern Britain* (Oxford, Oxford University Press, 1990), pp. 241–50.
9 Jonathan Glover, *Causing Death and Saving Lives* (Harmondsworth, Penguin, 1977), p. 27.
10 Stephen Klaidman and Tom L. Beauchamp, *The Virtuous Journalist* (New York, Oxford University Press, 1987), p. 19.

Chapter 2

Journalism in the market place

John O'Neill

A central argument of defenders of the free market is that freedom in the economic market is a necessary condition for democracy to flourish. The role of journalism and the press is central to this argument: they supply the link between the market and democracy.[1] A free market brings with it a free press that supplies the diversity of opinion and access to information that a citizenry requires in order to act in a democratic, responsible manner. The free market, journalism and democracy form an interdependent trinity of institutions in an open society. This liberal economic position has been prominent in recent debates concerning the First Amendment in the United States and the recent deregulation of the media in Europe.[2] In this paper I will attempt to prise these institutions apart. I will argue that, while journalism as a practice does have a necessary role in democratic societies, the market undermines the relation between journalism and democracy. There is a tension between the internal goals of journalism and the market contexts in which it operates; and the market inhibits the dissemination of information and diverse opinions required of a democratic society. In defending this position I will, for the most part, limit my discussion to journalism in a free market *per se*. Issues of monopoly in the press, while they are relevant to the points I raise, will not be discussed here.[3]

MARKETS, OWNERSHIP AND FREE SPEECH

Central to the argument for the free market in the field of journalism is that it ensures free speech. A free market is necessary for a free press and a free press is a central component of free speech. The view that a free press is simply a central application of a more general freedom of speech is a common one. On this view, for example, in the First Amendment to the Constitution of the United States – 'Congress shall make no laws . . . abridging the freedom of speech, or of the press' – 'freedom of the press' should be understood merely as a central instance of 'freedom of speech'. The amendment refers to one freedom, not two. However, the claim that a free press is simply one of the most important instances of free speech is mistaken, *if* by a 'free press' one means the freedom of a proprietor or editor to publish what they wish. This view of press freedom is presupposed by the Supreme Court's ruling on the *Miami Herald Publishing Co.* v. *Tornillo* case of 1974. In rejecting Tornillo's claim for space to reply to the *Miami Herald*'s attack on his character and candidature for state legislature, the court ruled that

> The choice of material to go into a newspaper, and the decisions made as to limitations of the size and content of the paper, and treatment of public issues and public officials – whether fair or unfair – constitute the exercise of editorial control and judgement.[4]

A point to note about this ruling is that the powers it refers to are not powers of free speech. They are, rather, powers to decide who has access to an organ of speech. To exercise such powers is not an exercise of a right of free speech as such, but of a power to decide who should use an organ for the exercise of a right to speech. In the Tornillo case, the paper had decided that a union leader should be denied such access. The freedom of the press is not in fact an instance of free speech, but refers, rather, to powers to control the speech of others. The question we must ask in considering the arguments for a free press, when it is thus defined in terms of editorial powers, is what legitimates such powers.

It is worth considering for a moment a parallel case of academic freedom and the powers of academic journals. Such journals have power over the access of academics to their pages. What legitimates such power is the process of peer review: papers submitted are selected for publication by placing them under the critical scrutiny of other members of the academic community who are competent to appraise the work. Such a system is not perfect – for example, there may be systematic biases against certain kinds of paper – but the process has a general legitimacy in that it appeals to a community of shared values and the acceptance, in general, of the competence of peers to judge the worth of a piece of work given such values.[5]

What legitimates editorial powers in the press? One possible answer is to appeal directly to property rights. Presses within the market place are private estates in print, and the editor has rights akin to those of any manager of a private estate in land – to include and exclude access to the estate. However, property rights provide a weak basis for the legitimation of the power to determine access to organs of speech, since they involve a restriction on the freedom of the propertyless.[6] While it is true that any editorial power entails restrictions, such exclusion of the propertyless, unlike the exclusion from academic journals of those whose work fails to meet certain internal standards, rests on no ethically significant boundaries which distinguish those with access from those without.[7] Correspondingly, just as there are good grounds for changing property rights in land to ensure the freedoms of the propertyless – either through use-rights within an area of private property, for example, rights of access by footpath; or forms of socialisation, for example, the creation of national trusts and parks – in so far as the power of editors is akin to those of private estate managers, there are good grounds for similar allowances for either use-rights within private estates in print, including rights of reply, for example, or the socialisation of such estates into public property. In so far as freedom of speech is concerned, socialised press estates may allow for greater possibilities for rights to use public organs for speech than do the private press estates that exist within a market system. Direct appeal to property rights fails to provide a satisfactory defence of editorial powers.[8]

However, there are other, more persuasive arguments for editorial rights of exclusion. It might be argued that the analogy between the editor and the manager of a private estate is an imperfect one, and that there are aspects in which his or her position can be closer to that of the peer-reviewer of an academic journal. Journalism is a practice with its own values and, relatedly, its own community structure. Systems of editorial control can reflect the judgements of peers within that community and in accordance with its values. Thus, while it may be the case that newspapers can turn into private fiefdoms of their owners, this need not be the case. And where it is the case, the goods of journalism are recognised to be in jeopardy. 'Editorial independence' has not been recognised. Hence the special arrangements and guarantees often involved in the ownership of newspapers in order to ensure such independence[9] and the special declarations owners sometimes make (although often with some cynicism) to respect editorial independence.[10] Such arrangements are, to be sure, precarious,[11] but where they do exist the legitimacy of editorial powers rests on something more than mere property rights. Rather, it reflects the judgements of an editor who accepts the internal goals and values of journalism. Thus, in defining a free press as one in which editorial independence is maintained, one is not appealing to property rights but to the internal goods of journalism.

This argument is not sufficient to support private property and a free market in the media. As we have just noted, editorial independence can often conflict with proprietorial rights. Moreover, it is not the case that private property is a necessary condition for such independence. However, having distinguished the legitimacy of editorial powers from those of property rights, the above argument might be conjoined to traditional liberal argument for a free market in the press, that the interests of democracy are best served by a press that is not socialised, but operates within a decentralised market system. Two points are commonly made in this regard. First, that market arrangements encourage a diversity of opinion and best serve the democratic need for an informed citizenry capable of passing judgements on the central issues that face them. Second, and relatedly, the market is the best institutional arrangement for ensuring that the press can act as a check on government, as a 'fourth estate' that checks the powers of the other three. In the rest of this chapter I address these arguments. In the next section I give a brief account of the goods of journalism, and argue that such goods are well suited to the democratic goals which the press is often taken to serve. However, in the following section, I argue that the goods of journalism are in tension with the requirements of the market place, and that the market place, far from providing an institutional arrangement in which the needs of democracy are served, is in conflict with them. While the practice of journalism and the needs of democracy are well suited to each other, the market is a friend of neither. I finish by examining the special pressures this tension places on the journalist.

THE PRACTICE OF JOURNALISM

Certain human practices – medicine and education for example – have internal ends which are partially constitutive of the kind of activity they are.[12] Journalism is among such practices. Just as health is an internal and constitutive end of medicine, so truth-telling about significant contemporary events is an internal and constitutive end of journalism.[13] As an end it distinguishes journalism from other practices akin to it, but distinct from it – for example those of pure entertainment. This is not to say that journalism always delivers the truth any more than it is true to say that medicine always delivers health. Rather, it is to say that where these practices do fail to deliver such goods, they fail in a special way. To criticise a doctor or medical institution for failing to provide adequate health care for patients is to make an internal criticism. It is to criticise them for failing to realise the very ends which the practice of medicine aims to serve. Likewise, to criticise a journalist, newspaper or radio or TV station for failing to report significant events truthfully is to accuse them of failing to perform that function constitutive of the practice. Thus while it is true that some doctors are bad doctors or that medical institutions may systematically fail to solve health problems – and perhaps even create them – it remains true that health as an end is constitutive of medicine.[14] Likewise, although some journalists may cease to report truthfully, and some newspapers may systematically distort the truth – or even become mere vehicles for entertainment produced by entertainers employing traditional journalistic skills[15] – it remains true that truth-telling is constitutive of journalism.

The same point can be made in another way. Consider what it is to be a cynical member of an occupation. To be a cynical journalist is to believe that truth-telling in journalism is a sham and that the practice is universally pursued for narrow self-interested aims. However, while the cynic does not believe that the goods of journalism are anywhere realised, either in his or her own work or that of others, the attitude presupposes a view of what the constitutive goods of journalism are supposed to be. The cynicism is parasitic on the acceptance of a shared view that the end of journalism is truth-telling. (I discuss the image of the cynical journalist further in the final section of this chapter.)

These constitutive ends of journalism also define the qualities characteristic of a good practitioner of the profession – the particular virtues and excellence of a journalist *as* journalist. Among these are those technical skills which are part of a journalist's craft – the ability to construct a story, to tell it well. However they also include broader ethical virtues which are associated with truth-telling – with the recognition and discovery of important truths and a willingness to report them. Thus typical virtues used by journalists to describe their peers are 'honest', 'perceptive', 'truthful'. Closely associated with these virtues of honesty and truthfulness is that of integrity – for example the sub-editor who insists on rewriting a front-page story to eliminate systematic bias in it. I return to this point in the final section.

Another, more contested, virtue that is often raised here is that of 'objectivity'. The virtue of 'objectivity' is often rejected by some of the best journalists of our day. Thus James Cameron writes that:

> I do not see how a reporter attempting to define a situation involving some kind of ethical conflict can do it with sufficiently demonstrable neutrality to fulfil some arbitrary concept of 'objectivity'. It never occurred to me, in such a situation, to be other than subjective, and as obviously so as I could manage to be. I may not always have been satisfactorily balanced; I always tended to argue that objectivity was of less importance than the truth, and that the reporter whose technique was informed by no opinion lacked a very serious dimension.[16]

I will not attempt to discuss the question of objectivity in detail here. However, two comments are in order. First, Cameron's rejection of objectivity stays within the circle of values of journalism. Objectivity is rejected in terms of a contrast with 'truth' and later with the need to present an account that can be 'examined and criticised' such that it will:

> encourage an attitude of mind that will challenge and criticise automatically, thus to destroy the built-in advantages of all propaganda and special pleading – even the journalist's own.[17]

The criticism of objectivity stays within the particular set of virtues associated with truth-telling. Second, and relatedly, the rejection of objectivity in journalism appeals to an argument that is accepted by traditional defenders of objectivity in the social sciences – notably by Weber – that if values are to enter into the reportage of empirical matters of fact, it is better that they do so explicitly rather than implicitly.[18] This has particular importance in journalism: given the degree to which the selection and presentation of news is value-laden, the critical faculties of the audience are better served by making those values explicit. 'Objectivity' in the sense of reportage which best allows the audience to appreciate the complexities of a situation may be better served by non-objective presentation of events.

Journalism, then, is a practice constituted by its own goods and a set of virtues among its practitioners that are necessary for the realisation of such goods. It follows from this that it makes sense to talk about a set of shared values to which journalists can appeal and – to return to the topic of the preceding section – such an appeal *might* be made to defend editorial independence. I say *might* here since it is not clear to me that editorial authority is the optimum way of enforcing those values – there are more democratic forms akin to peer-review that look more likely candidates – and the case for a more democratic internal structure to the press is a strong one. However, editorial control, where the editor recognisably enforces the internal values of journalism, does have a legitimacy which mere property rights do not.

However, the argument for a free press in the sense of the freedom of journalists to control the contents of their newspaper provides no argument for a free market in the media or for the private estates in print that such a market presupposes. In what follows I will argue that the market is systematically at odds with the values of journalism.

JOURNALISM IN THE MARKET AND THE FORUM

Journalism has traditionally been held to have a special role within democracies. The third Press Commission defined press freedom in terms of democratic responsibilities:

> We define the freedom of the press as that freedom from restraint which is essential to enable proprietors, editors and journalists to advance the public interest by publishing facts and opinions without which a democratic electorate cannot make responsible judgements.[19]

There are two components to the view that free journalism is a necessary condition for democracy. The first is that the media act as a watch-dog on government. Even where the press gains immense independent powers, it acts as a 'fourth estate' which provides a check on the other estates of government. The second is that the press is a necessary condition for an informed and critical citizenship. It provides information on major issues without which the public would not be able to make intelligent judgements. And it functions as a forum for public debate about such issues, serving to ensure that a diversity of opinions is heard.

It is clear that there is a necessary relation between the goods of journalism outlined in the last section and the functions that journalism is assumed to perform. Since truth-telling about significant contemporary events is constitutive of journalistic practice, where excellence in journalism exists, journalism will serve the creation of an informed and critical political citizenry. For the liberal, this happy alliance of journalism and democracy is best served by a free market. It is the market, unrestrained by political power, that provides the best institutional framework to ensure that the press satisfies those needs. However, I shall argue in what follows that, on the contrary, the market undermines journalism's capacity to provide for an informed and critical citizenry.

The disruption that the market causes to the relationship between journalism and democracy can be stated in general terms thus: to survive within the market place, the press has to satisfy the preferences of its consumers. As de Tocqueville puts it: 'A newspaper can survive only on the condition of publishing sentiments or principles common to a large number of men.'[20] However, this market imperative is incompatible with both the internal goods of journalism and the democratic function it is meant to serve. In the first place it is incompatible with the diversity which the market is claimed to engender: far from encouraging a diversity of opinion, the market place encourages the producer to present news in a way which is congruent with the pre-existing values and beliefs of its audience. It does not pay to present news which is outside the dominant cultural framework of the audiences addressed. Hence, mass journalism will tend to work within the confines of the dominant culture in which it operates. Relatedly, the value of truth-telling becomes at best subsidiary in the presentation of news. For it is not always the case that the truth about significant events is what the consumer prefers to hear or read. Indeed, the critical argument on which democratic debate depends often relies on the citizen's being informed of events and presented with views which he or she would prefer not to hear. What is portrayed in the press, how it is portrayed and how much it is portrayed is, within a free market, shaped by consumer preference. What *ought* to be portrayed, how it *ought* to be portrayed and how much it *ought* to be portrayed for the purposes of democratic discussion might be quite at odds with such preferences. Hence, while truth-telling might be constitutive of journalism *as* a practice, the free market entails that *in* practice it plays a quite subsidiary role. The 'news value' of a story is rarely a function of its truth value. It is, rather, a function of the perceived market at which the story is aimed.[21]

The market systematically shapes what is reported in a news story.

The consequence of this is not so much the reporting of falsehoods in the media – although this occurs[22] – but the failure to report what is of significance and a simplified presentation of events.[23] The democratic citizenry is rarely fully informed by the media that are supposed to serve it. Moreover, failure to report often results in the presentation of partial truths which, while not false in themselves, may set up implicatures among readers that are false. Something like the Gricean *principle of quantity*[24] assumed in standard conversation – that one supplies all relevant information – will convert partial truths into falsehoods. For example, to report a war solely in terms of conflict with a particular tyrant – which it may in part be – sets up implicatures that it is nothing but such a war – which is normally false. A free market in the press will tend to work against the ideal of an informed and critical citizenry. It rarely confronts its consumers with information, beliefs and knowledge which do not conform to their pre-existing preference – because it cannot afford to do so.

This market failure is compounded by similar economic pressures on the supply of information. Gathering information is costly, and there are pressures on newspapers to accept ready-made news stories from potential suppliers. Those with a particular viewpoint to present will effectively subsidise the media in the costs of gathering news – hence the growth of press agents and public relations officers. In doing so they are forced to present the press with versions of events that will sell within a particular market niche. This in turn infects democratic debate. Consider, for example, the differences within the Green movement concerning the activities of Greenpeace.[25] Greenpeace is highly effective in terms of media coverage. Its effectiveness is a consequence of its engaging in dramatic forms of action that make classically good news stories. It literally makes good 'news'. It carries with it the necessary camera equipment to ensure that it has good footage to pass on to the media – dramatic shots of small craft dwarfed by environmentally destructive giants, or of bloodstained white, large-eyed cuddly seals – and courts the journalists who cover their events. However, this approach poses problems for those who want a full democratic debate on the issues. The drama value of an issue may bear little relevance to its environmental significance. There is a danger that the environmental debate gets driven by an agenda which is set not in terms of the environmental importance of the issue but in terms of what makes for good publicity. As Yearly notes, the market encourages environmentalists

> to attend to what are perceived to be the most popular campaign themes; consequently the market reinforces the tendency for relatively unpopular issues to be marginalized. Such issues are nobody's favourite campaign topics even if the organizations privately regard them as important.[26]

The case of Canadian seals is a good example: in terms of either cruelty or endangered status there are more pressing cases which go unnoticed.

The problem of the economic constraints on news gathering also has a second consequence for the democratic functions of the press. The major subsidisers of news information are the governments over which the press is supposed to act as watch-dog. Through the lobby system in the United Kingdom and the system of press briefing in the United States, governments provide information on the cheap which is presented in a way that will yield maximal political benefits.[27] The media become heavily dependent on just those institutions on which they are taken to be a check. Moreover, like environmental groups, politicians will attempt to present information in a way that maximises its news value. The market in news shapes their presentation. The consequence is a deterioration of both democratic accountability and debate.

It might be objected that these arguments for the claim that the market distorts the relation of journalism and democracy depend on a number of assumptions about the preferences of consumers that are open to challenge. I have assumed that preferences are homogeneous, and hence that diversity of opinion is not served by the market. Moreover, I have assumed a particular content to such preferences – that there exists a widespread preference for simplified news, that there are few second-order preferences for one's existing preferences to be challenged, and so on. These objections have some power. Journalism and the market for news take place within a wider cultural, political and social context. Within particular periods of history and within particular social groups there can exist widespread preferences for news that is truthful and critical of accepted assumptions. Even given the absence of such self-critical preferences, the homogeneity assumption is weak. While it might be true, as de Tocqueville asserts, that 'a newspaper can survive only on the condition of publishing sentiments or principles common to a large number of men', it is not the case that such sentiments must be shared by *all* people. While each paper may not present its readers with unpalatable truths, what is palatable will differ across different groups in society. Hence, while there may be a conflict between the free market and a press that will function to create a critical and informed citizenry, there is no conflict between the market and diversity. Indeed, part of de Tocqueville's point was that in a pluralistic culture a diversity of association will encourage a diversity of opinion, whereas in a culture that has become homogeneous such diversity decreases. This claim is part of the central pessimistic message of *Democracy in America* concerning the growth of homogeneity and mediocrity. However, there is no reason to believe that de Tocqueville's picture of a mass homogeneous society has been realised. And given that it has not, the free market in the media is not incompatible with diversity.

A full response to these points would entail a detailed discussion of the relationship between markets, preferences and culture which is beyond the scope of this chapter. I confine myself here to two points of particular significance.

First, with respect to the assumptions about the content of preferences, while it is true that critical preferences can exist – and I do not want to suggest with theorists of mass society that it is impossible for the ordinary person to have such preferences – the problems of journalism and democracy need to start from where we are, that is, a context in which market-driven media do not appear to respond to such preferences. Moreover, the media cannot be treated as entirely passive agents in this regard. The media reproduce the preferences to which they respond. The difficulty in establishing critical media that accord with the ends of journalism is part of the problem of developing a critical political citizenry with preferences for the products of such media.

Second, with respect to the assumptions concerning homogeneity, there are limits to diversity. While modern societies may not be homogeneous, there are cultural and political boundaries within which most of the media operate. Diversity is circumscribed. Furthermore, diversity is limited by the nature of the markets in which the media operate. The commercial media exist in two markets: they sell their products to an audience and an audience to advertisers. Not all audiences are the same from the advertisers' perspective – only some form a potential market which it pays to address. A section of the population which has little purchasing power is in general less attractive to advertisers, and hence a newspaper that articulates its views will fail in its second market. Hence, the diversity of the press does not always reflect the diversity of a population. Thus, for example, the decline of the radical press in the UK has been a consequence not of a decline in readers – readership has sometimes increased during periods of decline – but rather of the lack of advertising revenue.[28] Likewise those minority groups which lack significant purchasing power lack a representative press. Advertising as a source of income limits diversity.

This said, within the constraints noted it is true that a limited diversity can be expected to arise from a free market. Furthermore, it is possible that such diversity sometimes serves some democratic ends. Where a government is seen to be opposed to some particular interest represented by a press, then one will expect criticism of that government via the media. Even given the state's power as a source of cheap news, the critical functions of the press undoubtedly do exist. What is badly served by the press is not the articulation of views opposed to that of an incumbent government, but the existence of an informed and critically engaged citizenry knowledgeable about the major issues that collectively face them.

A free market in the media serves a democracy, but a democracy of a particular kind. Democracy is served where it acts as a political market place. That is, in so far as democracy serves principally as a means of interest aggregation, acting in the manner of a surrogate market satisfying preferences in which votes serve as a surrogate currency, free-market media can serve as one means by which the perceived self-interests and opinions of particular groups are articulated, albeit those with greater purchasing power having a larger degree of influence. However, in so far as democracy is not a market but a forum in which informed citizens rationally debate those issues which face them, then the free market in the media serves democracy ill. While, properly constituted, journalism as a practice would serve that function, the market as an institutional framework for the media will tend to subvert the exercise of that function. Democracy as a forum is undermined by market-driven media.[29]

The arguments of this section are open to a final general response: while it may be true that market-driven media may not serve democracy as well as might be hoped, the alternative of media run from a centralised state will serve none of the functions demanded by democracy. The market, by decentralising power across different owners, is the only feasible framework in which a press capable of preserving democracy can exist.[30] This argument must be questioned, however. It reflects an assumption that is common in discussion of the market – that there exist just two feasible systems of information distribution: a centralised state-dominated system, or a decentralised market-led system. I have argued elsewhere that this dichotomy is a false one. Even within existing societies, non-market but state-independent and decentralised sources of information exist. The scientific community, for example, although it is now under market pressure, has traditionally relied on a decentralised but non-market institutional framework.[31] Within existing market societies such institutions exist with respect to the media, and I refer here not principally to public broadcasting institutions, but to other islands in which journalists have collectively attempted to realise journalistic practice, such as the Panos Institute.[32] Non-market, socialised and decentralised media serving the goals of both journalism and democracy as a forum are not a political impossibility.[33]

JOURNALISTS IN THE MARKET PLACE

> The specialised 'virtuoso', the vendor of his objectified and reified faculties, does not just become the [passive] observer in society: he also lapses into a contemplative attitude *vis-à-vis* the working of his own objectified and reified faculties . . . This phenomenon can be seen at its most grotesque in journalism. Here it is subjectivity itself, knowledge, temperament and powers of expression that are reduced to an abstract mechanism, functioning autonomously and divorced from both the personality of the 'owner' and from the material and concrete nature of the subject matter in hand. The journalist's 'lack of convictions', the prostitution of his experiences and beliefs is comprehensible only as the apogee of capitalist reification.[34]

A popular picture of the journalist is that of the hardened and cynical individual for whom nothing, not even the truth, counts against 'a good story'. (This is popular in fiction – see for example Mr Flack in Henry James's *The Reverberator* and Lousteau and the corrupted Lucien in Balzac's *Lost Illusions*.) I do not want to claim that this picture is a wholly accurate one – any more than is that of the prostituted journalist that Lukács draws. Lukács, like Balzac, tends to view journalists as corrupted poets, and fails to appreciate the internal ends of journalism. However, these pictures of the journalist highlight a real problem that the journalist faces. The journalist exists in two worlds: he or she enters a practice that is characterised by a commitment to truth-telling, and at the same time is an employee who works for a wage and is expected to produce a story of the kind demanded by his or her newspaper, magazine or TV station. The nature of such stories is determined by a market with which the journalist might have no sympathy.

These two demands on the journalist can clearly conflict. Where this occurs, the journalist exhibits vices and virtues characteristic of the trade. On the one hand, the conflict engenders a cynicism concerning the values constitutive of journalism and the divorce Lukács describes between the journalist's written word and his or her own beliefs and temperament. The journalist's personality and ethos are subverted by the dictates of his or her employee. On the other hand, in biographies of particular journalists, mention of the virtue of integrity is common. Such virtue is required not only in the peformance of a practice, but in resisting those external pressures which undermine its goods.[35] The history of journalism is full of examples of principled resignation by editors and journalists.[36]

The tension, then, between the practice of journalism and the market framework in which it operates produces characteristic virtues and vices. This is not to say that journalists fall into two classes – villains and heroes. Many, I suspect, find themselves forced to compromise the constitutive values of journalism, while at the same time insisting that some of the standards be enforced. The copy-editor may still have reservations about the final form of a story he or she has rewritten, yet be able in the process of rewriting to remove some of the bias, simplification and falsehood. While Lukács might be right in drawing attention to the special tension that exists for journalists between their beliefs and activities, that tension need not always be expressed in a 'lack of convictions' and the 'prostitution of his experiences and beliefs'. Journalists, like other workers, are not totally passive in their attitude to their own faculties. They also have the capacity to resist the pressures of the market place. The constitutive values of journalism have some power through such resistance, despite the countervailing tendencies of the market place.[37]

NOTES

1 See M. Friedman, *Capitalism and Freedom* (Chicago, University of Chicago Press, 1962), pp. 16ff. For a clear restatement of this position see D. Kelly and R. Donway, 'Liberalism and Free Speech', in J. Lichtenberg (ed.), *Democracy and the Mass Media* (Cambridge, Cambridge University Press, 1990), pp. 66–101.

2 See for example the recent collection of essays in Lichtenberg, *Democracy and the Mass Media*. On developments in Europe see D. McQuail and K. Siune (eds), *New Media Politics* (London, Sage, 1986).
3 For a discussion of these issues see J. Curran and J. Seaton, *Power Without Responsibility: The Press and Broadcasting in Britain*, 4th edn, (London, Routledge, 1991).
4 Cited in W. van Alstyne, *Interpretations of the First Amendment* (Durham, NC, Duke University Press, 1984), p.74.
5 I discuss these points in more detail in J. O'Neill, 'Property in Science and the Market', *The Monist*, 73 (1990), pp. 601–20. The publication of academic books is an interesting half-way house in this respect. It often employs similar peer-review mechanisms, but also brings external goals into play, in particular that of marketability. The size of the projected audience becomes more important.
6 See G.A. Cohen, 'Capitalism, Freedom and the Proletariat', in A. Ryan (ed.), *The Idea of Freedom* (Oxford, Oxford University Press, 1979), pp. 9–26, and 'Illusions about Private Property and Freedom', in J. Mepham and D. Ruben (eds), *Issues in Marxist Philosophy, Volume 4: Social and Political Philosophy* (Hassocks, Sussex, Harvester Press, 1981), pp. 223–42.
7 Thus while Gray is right to note against Cohen that all systems of property involve some restrictions on access, even if these might be voluntary (J. Gray, 'Against Cohen on Proletarian Unfreedom', *Social and Political Philosophy*, 6 (1989), pp.77–112), he fails to acknowledge the special problems with private property – that the boundary between those with and those without access is normally an ethically arbitrary one. In this regard it is interesting to note the way that owners of private property attempt to present themselves as guardians of particular values: for example, owners of land as agents of conservation. Such presentations are normally fairly flimsy.
8 There are of course a number of replies that might be made to the line of argument thus developed. For example, powers of exclusion from the press could be defended by reference to property rights on the grounds that those excluded have, within a market economy, the capacity to set up presses of their own. This argument fails for empirical reasons – it is simply false to say that all have the capacity within a market economy to reply through their own presses. (For example, the Third Royal Commission on the Press found that, in 1977, to establish a new local evening paper would cost between £2 million and £3 million: Royal Commission on the Press, Final Report, Cmnd 6810 (London, HMSO, 1977).) Other arguments in defence of private property in the media will be considered below.
9 See, for example, H. Evans, *Good Times, Bad Times* (London, Weidenfeld & Nicolson, 1983), chs 6–8.
10 Typical is Maxwell's statement on taking over the Mirror group: 'under my management editors will be free to produce their newspapers without interference with their journalistic skills and judgement' (cited in J. Pilger, *Heroes* (London, Jonathan Cape, 1986), p. 516).
11 See for example Evans, op. cit., pp. 400–5 and *passim* and Pilger,

op. cit., ch. 44 on failures to honour guarantees by Murdoch and Maxwell respectively.

12 This point is developed well by Aristotle: see Aristotle, *Nicomachean Ethics*, trans. T. Irwin, (Indianapolis, IN, Hackett, 1985), 1097b 25–7 and 1098a 8–15. See also Plato, *The Republic* trans. D. Lee, (Harmondsworth, Penguin, 1974), 342d 2–7. Compare A. MacIntyre, *After Virtue*, 2nd edn (London, Duckworth, 1985), ch. 14. For a more general discussion of the ways in which markets can undermine the constitutive goods of such practices see R. Keat, 'Consumer Sovereignty and the Integrity of Practices' in R. Keat and N. Abercrombie (eds), *Enterprise Culture* (London, Routledge, 1991), pp. 216–30.

13 For an argument that truth-telling should be an internal goal of the media quite generally, fictional as well as factual, see J. Mepham, 'Television Fictions: Quality and Truth Telling', *Radical Philosophy*, 57 (1991), pp. 20–7.

14 As Aristotle notes, the potentiality medicine has for the production of illness is derived from its primary function of health making (Aristotle, *Metaphysics*, ed. J. Barnes, *The Complete Works of Aristotle*, vol. 2 (Princeton, NJ, Princeton University Press, 1984), 1046b 4–15). The same point might apply to journalism concerning the relation of truth-telling and the actual production of falsehoods.

15 See for example Murdoch's telling comment during the Hitler diary hoax: 'we are in the entertainment business' (Evans, op. cit., p. 404). It is the case that some newspapers are no longer vehicles for the practice of journalism and are not perceived to be so – there is evidence for example that *Sun* readers are sceptical of the accuracy of what they read, while papers like the *Sunday Sport* are explicitly unconcerned with the truth value of that they 'report'. This distancing of newspaper production from the values of truth-telling and its recharacterisation as entertainment allows the easy relativism exhibited by Murdoch in his Edinburgh lecture of 1989 in which he identifies 'quality' with 'satisfaction of market preferences'. None of this is to deny the value of entertainment: it is rather to contest the claim that the practice of journalism can be treated purely as entertainment.

16 J. Cameron, *Point of Departure* (London, Grafton Books, 1969) p. 74. J. Pilger, 'A Question of Balance' in his *Heroes*, pp. 475–507, develops a similar position. For a different view that takes objectivity to be much closer to truth-telling than Cameron assumes see J.B. Abramson, 'Four Criticisms of Press Ethics' in Lichtenberg, op. cit., pp. 229–68.

17 Cameron, op. cit., pp. 74–5.

18 See M. Weber, *The Methodology of the Social Sciences*, trans. E. Shils and H. Finch (New York, Free Press, 1949).

19 Royal Commission on the Press, Cmnd 6810, op. cit., ch. 2, paragraph 3. Cf. Cameron, op. cit., p. 72.

20 A. de Tocqueville, *Democracy in America*, vol. II (New York, Knopf, 1945), p.113. Compare Balzac: 'Every newspaper is . . . a shop which sells to the public whatever shades of opinion it wants' (H. de Balzac, *Lost Illusions*, trans. H. Hunt, (Harmondsworth, Penguin, 1971) p. 314).

21 Cf. R. Entman, *Democracy Without Citizens* (Oxford, Oxford University

Press, 1989), and W.L. Bennet, *News: The Politics of Illusion*, 2nd edn (New York, Longman, 1988), ch. 1. For examples of the departure of news value from truth value see S. Cohen and J. Young (eds), *The Manufacture of News*, 2nd edn (London, Constable, 1981).

22 See for example Goldsmiths' Media Research Group, *Media Coverage of London Councils: Interim Report* (London, Goldsmiths' College, University of London, 1987).

23 Hence the standard complaints about modern journalism – that it decontextualises events, prefers news that fits standard narrative structures and presents it in these terms, personalises domestic and international politics, has a systematic bias towards European and American issues, and so on.

24 H. Grice, 'Logic and Conversation', in P. Cole and J.L. Morgan (eds), *Syntax and Semantics 3: Speech Acts* (New York, Academic Press, 1975), pp. 41–58.

25 For a good example of criticisms of Greenpeace on these grounds see E. Draper, 'The Greenpeace Media Machine', *New Internationalist*, no. 171 (May 1987), pp. 8–9. Related misgivings have been voiced by the publicity director of Greenpeace – see J. Porritt and D. Winner, *The Coming of the Greens* (London, Fontana, 1988), p. 94.

26 S. Yearly, *The Green Case* (London, Harper Collins 1991), p. 75.

27 On the Westminster lobby system see J. Tunstall, *The Westminster Lobby Correspondents* (London, Routledge & Kegan Paul, 1970); and J. Margach, *The Abuse of Power* (London, W.H. Allen, 1978). On the American context see L. Sigal, *Reporters and Officials* (Lexington, MA, Heath & Co., 1973).

28 See Curran and Seaton, op. cit., pp. 36–41, 95–9; and R. Williams, *The Long Revolution* (London, Chatto & Windus, 1961) p. 187f. and 'The Growth and the Role of the Media', in C. Gardner (ed.), *Media Politics and Culture* (London, Macmillan, 1979), pp. 14–24. Cf. F. Hirsch and D. Gordon, *Newspaper Money* (London, Hutchinson, 1975), and J. Keane, *The Media and Democracy* (Cambridge, Polity Press, 1991) pp. 81–8.

29 On the contrast between democracy as a market and democracy as a forum see J. Elster, 'The Market and the Forum', in J. Elster and A. Hylland (eds), *Foundations of Social Choice Theory* (Cambridge, Cambridge University Press, 1986), pp. 103–32.

30 See Friedman, op. cit, Ch. 1, and W. Evers 'Liberty of the Press under Socialism', *Social Philosophy and Policy*, 6 (1989), pp. 211–34 for a statement of this position.

31 See O'Neill, op. cit.

32 The Panos Institute is one of a number of small indpendent information gathering and dissemination agencies which includes journalists on its staff. It is particularly concerned with environmental and Third World issues.

33 For a development of this point see J. Keane, op. cit., pp. 144ff.

34 G. Lukács, *History and Class Consciousness* (London, Merlin Press, 1971), p.100.

35 See MacIntyre, op. cit., ch. 14.

36 For just two examples see the resignation of Gardner from the editorship of the *Daily News* in 1919 (S. Koss, *Fleet Street Radical*, London, Allen Lane, 1973, ch. 11) and Cameron's self-deprecating descriptions of his own departures from the *Daily Express* and the *Picture Post* (J. Cameron, op. cit., chs 5 and 9).

37 I would like to thank Roger Crisp, Russell Keat, Luke Martell and Yvette Solomon for their comments on an earlier version of this chapter; and Kelly Haggart, Glynn Roberts and William Outhwaite for their helpful conversations and suggestions.

Chapter 3

Owners, editors and journalists

Bruce Hanlin

THE ROBERT MAXWELL STORY

On Wednesday 6 November 1991, the *Daily Mirror* published one of the most extraordinary editions in its 88-year history. Early the previous day Robert Maxwell, 'Cap'n Bob', the newspaper's proprietor, had disappeared from the deck of his luxury motor yacht as it cruised around Tenerife in the Canary Islands. At teatime his 22-stone corpse was retrieved from the Atlantic and the *Mirror*'s obituary team swung into overdrive. Their efforts filled 15 complete pages in the 36-page tabloid that appeared on Wednesday morning. Maxwell was 'The man who saved the *Mirror*' according to a front-page headline that set the tone for an embarrassingly effusive tribute to a 'turbulent colossus', a 'publishing giant and world statesman' who was 'commander of every event in which he took part'.

Nothing really to match this had appeared in a national newspaper in Britain since the death of Winston Churchill in 1965. Indeed, Maxwell even outdid Churchill: he owned two League football clubs and the *Mirror*'s tribute rolled on into the sports pages. But there was something strangely missing from this eulogy. Every other commentary on Maxwell's death referred to the mounting financial difficulties facing his sprawling business empire. Only Maxwell's own papers stayed silent, and they could not remain so for long.

In addition to a 51 per cent stake in Mirror Group Newspapers in Britain, the Maxwell family held the controlling interest in Maxwell Communications Corporation (MCC), a publicly listed company whose world-wide operations included the American publishing house Macmillan. Alongside the public companies, and often interlinked with them in complex deals, there was a huge and complicated network of private Maxwell companies. These included two other newspapers: the *European*, launched in London in May 1990, and the New York *Daily News*, rescued from threatened closure in May 1991 with typical Maxwell razzamatazz.

The *Daily News* venture perfectly suited Cap'n Bob's talent for self-publicity, but it put an additional strain on a business empire that was already fatally overstretched with a growing mountain of unsupported debt owed to dozens of banks around the world. It is doubtful if the grand illusion could have been long maintained even with the chief conjuror still in control. With Maxwell's death a tangled web of illegal and semi-legal cash transfers, long-term 'stock lending', intergroup loans and share support schemes rapidly began to unravel.

To their horror *Mirror* journalists in London discovered within a month that their own company pension fund had been raided of at least £350 million, siphoned off through Maxwell private companies to cover their huge debts and to support the MCC share price. The aim was to mantain the asset value of Maxwell family stockholdings which had been pledged against yet further loans, sometimes apparently pledged to more than one lender at the same time. In all, MCC owed £1.4 billion to the banks; the Maxwell empire as a whole was more than £3 billion in debt; some £700 million of pension-fund money had simply vanished.

On Friday 6 December, a strap line across the bottom of the *Mirror*'s front page announced the inevitable: the Maxwell family's controlling stake was up for sale. The main headline, in 3½-inch type, said simply 'The Lie'. It referred specifically to assurances Robert Maxwell had given to the newspaper's finance director, a man whose office he had cynically bugged with hidden microphones. But symbolically that headline seemed to sum up the late proprietor's whole relationship with his staff and the corrosive influence he had had on the *Daily Mirror*'s journalism since his 'rescue' of the newspaper in July 1984. The grand obituary of a month earlier now looked like nothing so much as the sycophantic biographies another Maxwell subsidiary had published of various Eastern Bloc tyrants – Ceauşescu, Zhivkov, Honecker – before the revolutions of 1988–9 swept them away.

As the news focus began to shift to 'Maxwell's Missing Millions', to the folly of the international bankers who lent him vast sums on trust, and to the lax regulations that had enabled him to defraud his own work-force, editors and journalists who had worked for him were able to speak about the experience without fear of writs and injunctions. Robert Maxwell was not just another newspaper owner who enjoyed seeing his name in print. He was a supreme interventionist in almost every detail almost all the time, a bullying wheeler-dealer with the ethics of a black-market trader, whose monstrous ego steam-rollered over the protests and professional judgements of editors and executives alike.

As the liquidators moved in on the *European*, Simon Freeman, the paper's departing news-editor, recalled the experience of working for Cap'n Bob.[1] The *European* was Maxwell's personal project, launched as 'Europe's First National Newspaper' and supported by an open cheque-book, as well as desperately massaged circulation figures. From the start, the paper had suffered from a lack of identity and the all-too-palpable imprint of the proprietor's whims and innovations.

In the very first issue a page-one scoop about Soviet forces withdrawing from East Germany had been jettisoned at the last minute in favour of a boring, un-newsworthy and statistically worthless opinion poll conducted by yet another of Maxwell's companies. On another occasion the editor discovered to his astonishment that the *European* had a staff correspondent in the United States, hired personally by Maxwell during a visit to Israel some months earlier.

'The fact that the *European* survived as long as it did is testimony to the heroic efforts of its staff', says Freeman:

> It was constantly and confusingly 'relaunched': one day it was targetted at the club-class Euro-businessman who spoke English fluently; the next at a typical housewife in Toulouse, who could barely speak the language; the next at the *Daily Mail* reader in Britain. But the staff plodded on . . . The Cap'n was ever-present: on press day he would squeeze up the tiny, spiral staircase onto the editorial floor, commandeer a computer terminal and try to redesign the front page.[2]

The situation was not much different at the *Daily Mirror*. 'Could you produce the front page, if you had to?' Hugo Young asked Maxwell in a 1990 *Guardian* interview.[3] 'Not only could. I do', came the booming reply. 'Go and talk to the new editor. I'm rather good at designing front pages.' 'But you wouldn't want to interfere', persisted Young. 'I'm not shy of interfering if I have to. I'm not looking for it. But I could do the editor's job.' The boast would not have been so empty if Maxwell's journalistic instincts had been even a quarter as good as he imagined. Or if he had not specifically and repeatedly denied any intention of intervening editorially when he bought the *Mirror* and its stablemates in a controversial deal in 1984.

'Under my management, editors in the group will be free to produce their newspapers without interference with their journalistic skills and judgement', Maxwell had told a press conference on 13 July, the day after his bid was accepted.[4] There would be only two conditions: the papers would retain a broadly sympathetic approach to the labour movement, and would maintain a 'Britain first' policy.

If there was an echo of Beaverbook in the latter point it was in keeping with the image of the influential press baron that Maxwell had nurtured for himself for sixteen years and had finally attained. If, at the same time, there was any real commitment to 'sympathy for the labour movement' or to the ideal of editorial independence it was abandoned before the month was out.

On 26 July 1984 Maxwell substantially changed a by-lined column on the miners' strike then in progress that had been written by Geoffrey Goodman, the *Mirror*'s industrial editor. Confronted by the angry journalist the following morning, the new proprietor turned on the charm, issued further promises of strict non-intervention in the future, and somehow persuaded Goodman not to resign. Part of the bargain was that he would in future send his articles in advance for Maxwell to read. He was not the only *Mirror* journalist to succumb, for a time at least.

Maxwell clearly saw himself as the peacemaker in the coal dispute, but when his suggestions were rejected by Arthur Scargill, the miners' leader, he very quickly lost patience and enlisted the newspaper in support of his own version of events. David Seymour, a leader-writer with thirteen years standing at the *Mirror*, later described how Maxwell inserted himself into the editorial process so that writing the '*Mirror* Comment' column became a matter of negotiation with the proprietor, conducted in competition with an unending stream of phone calls in any of Maxwell's eight languages with stockbrokers, currency dealers, property consultants, and football-club managers. In the midst of all this, the attempt to adhere to established journalistic values such as accuracy, fairness and factual truthfulness soon went the way of Maxwell's promises of non-interference.[5]

Maxwell inserted himself, quite literally, into other areas of the paper, too. For the first year of his involvement, the *Mirror* that had once campaigned fiercely on political and social issues came instead to resemble a Maxwell family album, studded with photographs of Cap'n Bob and filled with references to other companies within the group, in which five of his children were, in due course, employed. Journalists began to drift away from the paper, readers abandoned it in droves. It was all a long way from the halcyon days of the 1960s, to which critics increasingly referred, when the newspaper was riding high with a mammoth circulation and no effective rival.

If there was any counterbalancing factor, it lay in Maxwell's impact on the production side. At the British Printing Corporation he had faced down the powerful printing unions and forcefully imposed new processes and new manning agreements. He made it clear he was quite prepared to do the same at the *Daily Mirror*, which like the rest of Fleet Street in the early 1980s was a redoubt of hot-metal technology, overmanning and extravagant 'old Spanish practices'. At his first meeting with the *Mirror* printers Maxwell told them bluntly: 'I have invested £90 million in this business and I don't belong to the Salvation Army. I am the proprietor. I am the boss.'[6] This was not a challenge to endear him to the labour movement, particularly with the newspaper's traditional sympathies, but it was arguably a necessary step in restoring the fortunes of an increasingly moribund company. And, in fact, Maxwell accomplished the change to new technology in the Mirror Group with far less open bloodshed than his arch rival Rupert Murdoch at News International.

OWNERSHIP AND ETHICS

Many critics might agree with the suggestion that any man rich enough to buy a newspaper should not be allowed to own one, but within the current limits of the law few could disagree that ownership of the Mirror Group gave Maxwell every right to tell his printers how he intended to manage the company. From an ethical standpoint, however, the issue becomes more problematic when rights of ownership are extended to the editorial sphere.

Whatever his public promises, did Maxwell's role as 'publisher' convey the right to act as *de facto* editor-in-chief? What conventions separating the role of owners from those of their editors and journalists did he transgress? What course of protest was open to the journalists? Should, or could, a distinction between management and editorial functions be enforceable by law or in some other way? Can the question, in any case, be separated from the wider issues of monopoly ownership, of political influence, and of the role of the press and other media in a democratic society?

If the long saga of Robert Maxwell's involvement with the *Daily Mirror* was an isolated incident such questions could safely be left in a footnote. However, in Britain the concept of 'press freedom' has a chequered past and an ambiguous present, and remains fundamentally a right to publish: a property right attached to ownership, not a charter for editorial independence. The individual owner who adopts a strictly non-interventionist approach is a rare figure indeed. Robert Maxwell may have been 'larger than life' both physically and figuratively, and in view of the subsequent financial scandals he might be said to have been larger than death too, but as a 'hands-on' newspaper proprietor he was no great exception to the rule.

The model of the Fleet Street press baron was established no later than the years immediately after the First World War. Northcliffe, with *The Times* and the *Daily Mail*, and Beaverbrook with the *Daily Express*, engaged in a relentless pursuit of political influence which saw their detailed personal control over their newspapers extend to cover the general content, news values, layout and day-to-day administration as well as the political opinion columns. Their staff became used to working through a constant barrage of telephone calls, urgent instructions and cantankerous memos.

After Northcliffe's death in 1922, his brother, Lord Rothermere, joined with Beaverbrook in an attempt to set a policy agenda for the Conservative government that led ultimately to Baldwin's famous 1931 denunciation of them for seeking 'power without responsibility'.[7] Such action by newspaper owners was clearly an infringement of the democratic process. But when, sixteen years later, an unrepentant Beaverbrook cheerfully told the first Royal Commission on the Press that he ran his newspapers 'purely for the purpose of making propaganda, and with no other object',[8] was he guilty of an equivalent ethical breach or merely exercising his rights as a proprietor?

In May 1968, Cecil Harmsworth King, Northcliffe's nephew and the chairman of Daily Mirror Newspapers, took a fateful step along the path followed by Beaverbrook and Rothermere in 1931: he wrote and published a signed editorial under the title 'Enough is Enough' calling for the resignation of the Labour prime minister, Harold Wilson, and his replacement by a 'neutral' figure.[9] The editors of the various group papers were only asked for their opinion on the article after it had appeared: they dutifully offered their support, but this was hardly enough. King's statement was completely ineffective politically, and disastrous personally, as he was not a traditional proprietor but merely the chairman of a company responsible to its board of directors. He was duly fired, though for endangering the company's relationship with the government rather than for a blatant infringement of the convention covering the publisher–editor relationship.

In 1969, Rupert Murdoch, then an unknown Australian newspaper owner, made his first appearance on the British media stage when the Carr family ownership invited his investment in a declining *News of the World*, not least to hold off the predatory advances of Robert Maxwell. Murdoch immediately began to reorganise the paper, and when the startled editor protested told him bluntly: 'I did not come all this way not to interfere.'[10]

Within six months Murdoch had gained full ownership control of the Sunday *News of the World*. Within nine months he had bought the struggling daily *Sun* for a bargain price and relaunched it as a brash, down-market tabloid that was soon overtaking the *Daily Mirror* as Britain's most popular newspaper. This was the start of Murdoch's international media empire. As it has grown, more and more control has been delegated to local executives and trusted individual editors, but it is a notable feature of Murdoch's management approach that he has never stopped 'interfering' with the style, content and politics of his various newspapers, magazines and television companies around the world.

In 1977, thirteen years after the death of Beaverbrook, the ailing *Daily Express* group was bought by the property and construction company Trafalgar House. Victor (later Lord) Matthews, who had spent his working life in the building trade, became chairman and rapidly assumed the posture of a press baron, though previously he had cheerfully confessed to rarely reading more than the racing pages of any paper and to never reading the quality press at all.[11] In what he clearly thought were reassuring words on the subject of journalistic independence he famously told one questioner: 'By and large the editors will have complete freedom as long as they agree with the policy I have laid down.'[12]

Other owners may have been more circumspect, but Matthews was only reasserting the traditional right of the proprietor as he saw it. In his case, though, the 'approved policy' took some alarming shifts as his lack of interest in editorialising gave way to active and eccentric involvement. On one occasion the editor of the *Evening Standard* had to dissuade Matthews from using the paper to call for a nuclear strike on Moscow to rid the world of communism. Meanwhile at the *Express* five editors in seven years struggled without success to halt a decline in circulation, while coping with the proprietor's lengthy political discourses and suggestions for editorials in support of patriotism, the royal family and Conservative party policies.

One of those many editors was Derek Jameson, a lifelong Labour voter and a deputy editor of the *Daily Mirror* when Matthews offered him the job in 1977. Jameson told him that while it was flattering to be approached his personal politics hardly agreed with the *Express*'s uncritical support for the Conservatives. 'That doesn't matter', Matthews told him. 'You wouldn't be stupid enough to try to turn a Tory paper into a Labour newspaper.'[13] This compliment to Jameson's professionalism was also an invitation to him to censor his own political opinions.

After reflection Jameson accepted the job, arguing that after a long career in popular newspapers he could hardly refuse an editorship, even on a Tory paper, particularly since no vacancy was in sight on the Labour-supporting *Mirror*. Such problems, of course, did not apply the other way around. Matthews saw no difficulty in trying to turn the *Express*'s down-market stablemate the *Daily Star* into a Tory paper, even though the sympathies of its editor, its staff and most of its potential readers lay with Labour.[14]

The quality press were not immune from disputes between editors and proprietors, either, and the two most public rows of the early 1980s occurred for different reasons at *The Times* and the Sunday *Observer*. At the centre of these were Rupert Murdoch, the most powerful of modern press barons, and 'Tiny' Rowland, the chief executive of Lonrho and another businessman turned proprietor.

In 1981, Murdoch acquired *The Times* and *The Sunday Times* in a controversial deal that united the country's most prestigious daily and its best-selling quality Sunday with the *Sun* and the *News of the World*, the circulation leaders in the popular press. This broke the established monopolies and mergers rules on newspaper ownership, and appeared to have been sanctioned by the new Conservative government as a 'reward' to Murdoch for the support he had given to the party in the 1979 general election.

The two quality titles had been brought under the same ownership by Roy (later Lord) Thomson in 1966, and for a decade had enjoyed the benign control of a man who enjoyed the prestige of ownership without seeking to exercise the power of proprietorship. Lord

Thomson, however, had died in 1976, and his son and successor was determined to move the papers into the electronic age with a plan partially to computerise production. This, of course, was a direct challenge to the entrenched position of the company's printers.

In the ensuing dispute the newspapers were, remarkably, closed down for almost a year between December 1978 and the following November, during which time various ideas for alternative structures were floated, including possible schemes for a journalist-led co-operative buy-out. In the event, Times Newspapers settled on terms virtually dictated by the print unions, and as costs and losses continued to mount, the Thomson Organisation put the company up for sale.

Murdoch was not the only potential purchaser, though as history has confirmed he was the one most likely to succeed where Thomson had failed in challenging traditional Fleet Street production practices. Initially, however, Murdoch had to overcome the political row that greeted his deal. The powers of watch-dog 'independent directors' were reaffirmed, and guarantees of complete editorial freedom were given. To substantiate his good intent Murdoch invited Harold Evans, the long-serving, award-winning and highly esteemed editor of *The Sunday Times* to take over and invigorate its daily counterpart.

Within a year the cynical nature of the new proprietor's promises became clear. Instructions on the selection and balance of news and opinion flowed in to the editor, often transmitted from New York or other locations, as Murdoch attempted to shift the political line of *The Times* by reducing or removing criticism of the Thatcher government. When Evans resisted, the pressure intensified. Executive control was tightened over all editorial expenditure, breaking another of Murdoch's promises, and the proprietor began to intrigue against his editor. Eventually Evans resigned. The independent directors' 'watch-dog' powers proved inadequate to deal with a 'voluntary' departure.[15]

By 1985 both *The Times* and *The Sunday Times*, under editors who shared Murdoch's political attitudes, had been enrolled alongside his strident tabloids in a campaign for the 'deregulation' of British broadcasting. Editorial opinion columns and sensationalised news stories carried attacks against the BBC in particular and the idea of public service broadcasting in general. These served a dual purpose. Murdoch was about to launch his four-channel Sky-TV satellite service; his friend the Prime Minister, Margaret Thatcher, was at the height of her 'free-market' zeal.

It was all a long way from the days of Roy Thomson, when each newspaper was free to establish and hold its own opinion without reference to the proprietor, who always insisted:

> 'I do not believe that a newspaper can be run properly unless its editorial columns are run freely and independently by a highly skilled and dedicated professional journalist. This is and will continue to be my policy.'[16]

The clash with Murdoch at Times Newspapers might have been fought earlier and on different ground; instead the *Observer* found crises of a different sort. In 1976, the year Thomson died, Murdoch was actually invited to take control of the liberal and independent, but financially weak, Sunday paper. In the event, amid strong opposition from the staff, the offer was withdrawn in favour of the unlikely philanthropy of Atlantic Richfield, an American oil company based in Los Angeles. Four years and some $20 million later, the paper was passed on to another wealthy conglomerate seeking a prestige outlet: Tiny Rowland's Lonrho International, which owned a group of newspapers in Scotland and had extensive interests in Africa.

The clash between Rowland and Donald Trelford, the *Observer*'s editor, when it came in April 1984, centred on these trading connections rather than British domestic politics. Trelford published a full-page report alleging atrocities by the army in Zimbabwe, where Lonrho companies earned some £15 million profit annually. Rowland cabled an immediate apology to Robert Mugabe, the Zimbabwe president, and sternly rebuked Trelford. When the editor rejected the complaint of inaccuracy Rowland threatened to withdraw all Lonrho's advertising from the *Observer*, and held an ostentatious meeting with Robert Maxwell to discuss a possible sale of the paper.

On this occasion brinkmanship failed. The editor was backed unanimously by the journalistic staff, while the paper's five independent 'watch-dog' directors denounced Rowland for 'improper proprietorial interference' and gave Trelford their full support for 'vigorously maintaining his editorial freedom and defending his professional integrity'.[17] A face-saving formula was devised to resolve the dispute and Trelford remained as editor. However, subsequent events suggest his autonomy and freedom of action did not survive intact.

Throughout the 1980s Tiny Rowland was deeply embroiled in an obsessive dispute of byzantine complexity over the ownership of Harrods, the famous Knightsbridge store. Lonrho's attempt to buy the House of Fraser stores group had, he claimed, been thwarted with the collusion of the Department of Trade and various ministers in the Thatcher government, who had favoured a bid by the Fayed brothers, three Egyptians of somewhat dubious wealth and background. It was inevitable that the *Observer* would get entangled in this dispute.

On Thursday 30 March 1989, in a blatant publicity stunt, this Sunday paper published a 'special edition' devoted entirely to Lonrho's legal case which was being considered that afternoon by the House of Lords. Needless to say, this expensive gesture owed little to journalistic news values or editorial initiative. Only a few hundred copies were sold before the issue was declared to be in contempt of court, and the episode can hardly be seen as anything other than proprietorial abuse of the newspaper's name and reputation.

At the same time an equally damaging argument was rumbling through the *Observer*'s news-room. Lonrho's world-wide connections have often given the paper privileged access to business and diplomatic circles, and though Trelford has always insisted that Rowland's tip-offs and initiatives are assessed purely on their journalistic merits his staff reporters have often felt uneasy. Matters came to a head in 1989 over a story alleging that British Aerospace had been paying huge bribes to clinch the sale of Tornado fighter aircraft to Saudi Arabia. The information came from a German business contact of Rowland's, whom Trelford met when he accompanied a high-level Lonrho delegation to Iran in January.

Back in London, David Leigh, the *Observer*'s associate editor and key investigative reporter, refused to touch yet another 'Lonrho implant'. In his account of the episode, the dossier was hawked around the newspaper's offices for several weeks as journalist after journalist refused to handle it or found the unsourced information would simply not stand up. Meanwhile pressure was building on the editor to give it his highest priority, and two stories written by a senior executive did eventually appear in the paper in March. Leigh took his complaints of direct proprietorial influence to the *Observer*'s National Union of Journalists branch, and from there to the independent directors.

This 'court of appeal' decided there was nothing to support the charges. Trelford, in a statement to the directors, insisted that the story was in the public interest, that Lonrho's connection had never been concealed, that *Observer* reporters had been free to decline the assignment and had not suffered professionally for doing so. He denied there had been pressure from Rowland, or any commercial gain for Lonrho.[18]

Leigh felt that the independent directors' decision was only a whitewash. He resigned from the newspaper and later went to work for Thames Television's *This Week* programme. 'I felt ashamed' he wrote in the *Guardian*:

> This was not journalism as I knew it, and it was not the *Observer* I had originally gone to work for. I felt it had become a sick newspaper. How could I write stories exposing conflicts of interest in MPs and businessmen, when no-one seemed sufficiently concerned about potential conflicts of interest in my own newspaper?[19]

On Fleet Street, history not infrequently repeats itself, first as tragedy, then as farce. On 16 June 1991 the *Observer* carried a short 'Letter from Malawi' by Julie Flint, a well-regarded journalist. In a jocular style the piece referred to the somewhat bizarre attempts to impose a 'moral code' on the country by the ageing and increasingly eccentric Life President, Dr Hastings Banda, who was also quick to lock up any potential dissidents. The following week the newspaper carried an apology regretting 'any errors contained in our report', plus a long rebuttal by one of Banda's political associates, plus a hurt letter from the Malawi ambassador in London. On 30 June yet another, even more fulsome, apology appeared, addressed personally to the Life President. Lonrho, of course, still has an important agricultural and commercial involvement in Malawi. For the *Observer* it all seems a long way from the days of 1984.

Or is there a more Machiavellian explanation, as offered by Robin Morgan, a former *Sunday Express* editor, in a comment on this latest *Observer* story?[20] Was it a calculated risk by Trelford to show Rowland that nothing was 'off limits', even if the price was a grovelling apology later? Other critics might not be so generous, and would offer only qualified support for Morgan's other contention that 'most proprietors concede a considerable amount of independence to editors and invest millions in their instincts and views with only one condition – circulation success'.[21]

PRESS FREEDOM: WHOSE FREEDOM?

Proprietors invariably seek to safeguard their position through the appointment of an editor who shares, or at least accepts, their opinions on general policy, even if differing on detail. Ideally, the task of the editor is to ensure that this general policy is followed, but without calling upon journalists to write in conflict with their own principles or knowledge of the facts. In practice 'editorial independence' may be largely limited to day-to-day matters of style, content and the editorial budget, rather than 'strategic' decisions on political alignment or major issues, which are usually settled by the proprietor.

At the same time, the fiercer the battle for circulation the greater the commercial pressures on editors to erode journalistic standards on matters of truth, accuracy and ethical acceptability. Commercial decisions on marketing, the publisher's responsibility, easily overlap with editorial requirements. The greater the prestige or circulation of the paper, the greater the attraction for a proprietor with strong opinions seeking a 'megaphone', as Maxwell bluntly called his *Daily Mirror.*

While editors certainly bear the brunt when relations with proprietors are rough, ordinary staff journalists usually have little scope to challenge the policy of the paper on political or ethical grounds even in normal circumstances. In the normal news-room procedure, particularly in the popular press, stories from reporters are collated and rewritten for publication by sub-editors and the 'back bench' of senior editorial executives. Political edges can be smoothed, new 'facts' inserted, the angle of the story subtly changed. Even before this, the selection of stories to be covered and their assignment to particular journalists can ensure that the political line decided by the proprietor or the presentational angle determined by the editor can be imparted without direct instruction.

If difficulties do arise and cannot be resolved in discussion with the editor, reporters have only two choices: to resign or to remove their by-line from the published story. Resignation is, not surprisingly, very much a last resort; pragmatic acceptance of the status quo is the way to self-preservation and the safeguarding of employment prospects, at least unless provocation reaches a peak. Producing a newspaper is a team operation played out under immense pressure, conditions in which 'professionalism' may easily substitute for more abstract issues of 'principle'.

Even a proprietor like Maxwell, well known for seeing himself as team captain, coach and referee rolled into one, was able to assemble a team prepared to play by his rules. Some journalists undoubtedly found his unpredictability exciting and his appeals to their self-esteem gratifying, as the *Mirror*'s obituary issue subsequently demonstrated. For others it was very different. Roy Greenslade was an 'outsider' brought in as editor in January 1990, knowing the score but attracted by the prestige of the job and 'a mixture of innocence and arrogance: I considered that none of the stories could have been as bad as the tellers made out, and if they were I thought I was the man to prove the others wrong'.[22]

Greenslade lasted 14 months in the job, during which he gained solid support from the *Mirror*'s journalists for tightening up the news and political coverage and restoring some of the old campaigning spirit.[23] He describes this time as a period of constant skirmishing with Maxwell: 'making accommodations, hedging, dissembling, retreating . . . a continual battle of tactics to circumvent the beast on the 10th floor'.[24] Eventually he was fired, without apparent reason or explanation, but since his formal contract of employment had still not been signed, Maxwell was able to extract an 'oath of silence' from Greenslade as the price of his pay-off, and to threaten him with writs if he ever mentioned their disagreements.

For those journalists on the *Mirror* committed to addressing social and political issues from a left-wing perspective the choices were always stark: to leave the paper, as did Geoffrey Goodman, David Seymour and John Pilger; or to remain, like the columnist Paul Foot, in the hope of achieving something in spite of the need for careful self-censorship. Despite the editorial distortions of recent years, Mirror Group Newspapers remain the only section of the mass circulation popular press to support the Labour Party.

Throughout most of the 1980s their competitors, reflecting the right claimed by proprietors to 'make propaganda' as they chose, provided a celebration rather than any critical examination of the Conservative government's actions. At the same time, under the impetus of those same proprietors, intense competition for market share relentlessly devalued journalistic values in pursuit of formulaic sensationalism and frivolous entertainment.

Sections of the quality press – the *Guardian*, *The Independent*, the *Financial Times* – have nobly maintained a public interest role, but in a changing and increasingly complex democratic society there is a need for diversity of values and perspectives that is ill-served by the current range of national newspapers. The press has a dual function to perform, as both public institution and private industry. Editorial independence is essential to underpin its role as watch-dog on government and business affairs, as provider of the information on which democratic decisions can be fairly made, and as the representative of public opinion and community values. At the same time, history has shown that profitability provides the best underpinning for editorial independence: the survival of the press as a democratic institution depends upon its survival as an industry.

The ideal, perhaps, as *The Independent* somewhat piously suggested in a comment on the impending change of ownership at the *Daily Mirror*, is for newspapers to be owned by people solely interested in seeing an economic return on their investment. Those who acquired titles for reasons other than profit, the paper's leader column argued, inevitably used their purchases to peddle political and commercial influence.[25] If the political will should ever be forthcoming there is no shortage of proposals for a radical restructuring of the press by breaking up the present heavy concentration of ownership and providing funding for new initiatives through a central funding agency.[26] Such proposals challenge the conventional idea of 'press freedom' as a property right. This is the first stage in reassessing the ethical obligations of proprietors.

NOTES

1 *Guardian*, 13 December 1991.
2 ibid.
3 *Guardian*, 5 March 1990.
4 Cited in Tom Bower, *Maxwell: The Outsider*, rev. edn (London, Mandarin Books, 1991), p. 382.
5 Bower, ibid. Chapter 13 covers Maxwell's take-over of Mirror Group Newspapers. See also Mark Hollingsworth, *The Press and Political Dissent* (London, Pluto Press, 1985), ch. 8; and John Pilger, *Heroes* (London, Jonathan Cape, 1986), ch. 42.
6 Cited in Bower, op. cit., p. 381.
7 For a survey of Fleet Street history see, for example, James Curran and Jean Seaton, *Power Without Responsibility: The Press and Broadcasting in Britain*, 4th edn (London, Routledge, 1991); or Simon Jenkins, *The Market For Glory* (London, Faber & Faber, 1986).
8 *Royal Commission on the Press 1947–49, Minutes of Evidence, 26th Day*, Par 8656, Cmnd 7416.
9 *Daily Mirror*, 10 May 1968.
10 Cited in Curran and Seaton, op. cit., p. 81.
11 Jenkins, op. cit., p. 128.
12 Cited in Jenkins, ibid., p. 129.

13 Cited in Hollingsworth, op. cit., p. 23.
14 ibid., pp. 231–6.
15 Harold Evans, *Good Times, Bad Times* (London, Weidenfeld & Nicolson, 1983), gives a detailed account of his years working with Thomson and his clash with Murdoch.
16 Quoted in Evans, ibid., p. 491.
17 *Observer*, 22 April 1984.
18 More pertinent than any commercial gain for Lonrho, perhaps, was an opportunity for Rowland to embarrass both Professor Roland Smith, chairman of British Aerospace but formally of House of Fraser, and the Department of Trade and Industry.
19 *Guardian*, 3 July 1989.
20 *Guardian*, 15 July 1991.
21 ibid.
22 *The Sunday Times*, 8 December 1991. Greenslade was brought in when Maxwell proposed to float the *Sunday People* as an independent company headed by Richard Stott, editor of the *Mirror*. Characteristically, Maxwell later changed his mind. Stott resumed as editor of the *Mirror* when Greenslade departed.
23 Ironically, the major *Mirror* investigation published during Greenslade's tenure had all the hallmarks of Maxwell settling a grudge. A series of articles in March 1990, based on an inquiry begun under Stott, claimed that National Union of Mineworkers' funds had been fraudulently misused by the union president, Arthur Scargill, during the coal dispute five years earlier. Though it won a British Press Award this 'investigation' in fact relied on 'cheque-book journalism' and uncorroborated evidence from a convicted fraudster. See Campaign for Press and Broadcasting Freedom, *Free Press*, no. 64, June 1991.
24 *The Sunday Times*, 8 December 1991. Roy Greenslade, *Maxwell's Fall* (London, Simon & Schuster, 1992), gives a graphic account of his time with Cap'n Bob.
25 *The Independent*, 10 December 1991. On 7 January 1992 it was announced that the *European* had been bought by David and Frederick Barclay, two reclusive bothers resident in Monaco who appeared to have no wish to adopt the trappings of proprietorship.
26 See for example, James Curran, 'Mass Media and Democracy: A Reappraisal', in J. Curran and M. Gurevitch, *Mass Media and Society* (London, Edward Arnold, 1991), pp. 82–117; Campaign for Press and Broadcasting Freedom, *Free Press*, no. 65, July 1991.

Chapter 4

Freedom of speech, the media and the law

David Burnet

You praise the firm restraint with which they write
I'm with you there, of course:
They use the snaffle and the curb all right
But where's the bloody horse?[1]

According to Article 10 of the European Convention on Human Rights 'Freedom of speech should only be restricted where there is a pressing social need to do so for the advancement of some other important objective'. Such freedom may be subject to conditions prescribed by law and 'necessary in a democratic society in the interests of national security'. The recent history of official secrets law and related legal constraints in the UK is to a lamentable extent, and in spite of patriotic rhetoric and executive double-talk about 'liberalisation', one of increasing encroachment on freedom of speech and disregard for the aspirations expressed in the convention. To be strictly accurate, the high-water mark of oppression and suppression was probably recorded a few years ago, as for instance with the outbreak of injunctivitis[2] in late 1987, or with the passage of legislation in 1989, and the present predicament is more one of contemplating life after death.

Focusing on legal constraints, however pervasive, in isolation is clearly artificial. Unfortunately, in the UK, journalists and others faced with the task of expanding their knowledge (and critical capacity) in the shrinking confines of defensible legal space have also to contend with a bewildering variety of complementary and competing extra-legal constraints. These include the timeworn political climate of obsessional secrecy, the D-Notice informal constraints, the problems of attributable and non-attributable 'leaks' and of authorised communication in general. All of which leads to the cliché born of cynicism that the extent of institutional secrecy is itself a secret. Similarly, under recent legislation, in many cases the revelation of criminality is itself a criminal offence.

It is hardly a coincidence that the Thatcher era produced a flurry of legislative activity in this area, most notably the Official Secrets Act 1989 and the Security Service Act 1989, but no sign of Freedom of Information legislation. The existing criminal law proved unsatisfactory in such cases as *Ponting*[3] and in any event tends to operate *ex post facto*. Just as significant, however, has been the achievement of the judiciary (with some exceptions, usually among the lower ranks) in fashioning the civil law of confidence and the criminal law of contempt in concert so far as to vie with the executive in tightening the noose on freedom of expression for journalists and the media in general. In all these developments traditional defences such as prior publication or public interest have been eroded or extinguished by the legislature (as in the Official Secrets Act 1989) or by the judiciary (as in the *Spycatcher* litigation).

A particularly ominous development is the availability of interlocutory (pre-trial) injunctions for breach of confidence against specific publishers of information, backed up by the use of the law of contempt against any other publisher – in essence blanket suppression via 'gagging' writs. Domestic UK law has experienced no difficulties in creating this network of suppression, and the only mechanism for change is likely to be in response to decisions of the European Court of Human Rights, in respect of both the availability of pre-trial injunctions and conceivably the substantive law of confidence itself.

MY COUNTRY RIGHT OR WRONG

In a climate of sterile secrecy, uncertainty and ideological ferment who can decide what information properly falls (or is pushed) into the public domain and what legitimately lies behind the curtain of national security? The media are no nearer finding the Archimedean point than anyone else. However the commonsensical point of view, and one commonly held and acted on in liberal democracies, is that expressed by Roy Hattersley in the debates on the recent Official Secrets Bill – that:

> In a free society, official secrets legislation should protect information that, were it to become widely available, would jeopardise the security of the nation. It should not however

> embrace . . . information that can be made public without damaging the national interest, whether or not the publication of that information embarrasses the Government of the day.[4]

Mutatis mutandis, this principle can be applied to judicial weighing of conflicting public interests. But its practical implementation is beset with difficulties, especially in the UK. Who is to decide on the question of harm to the national interest? The choice ranges from ministerial certificate through Information Commissioner to judge and jury. The current problem for the media in a democracy less than liberal with information is to keep the notional demarcation lines in focus, since by definition the task of distinguishing necessary from expedient secrecy is frequently dependent on official information, convenient leaks, etc., against a background of legal constraint.

At any rate some of the judiciary, for example, Mr Justice Scott in *Spycatcher*,[5] endorse the proposition that a balance must be struck between the interests of national security and the freedom of the press. The metaphor of the balance gives an air of objectivity to the irreducibly subjective activity of evaluating 'public interests'. It is true that 'weighing' is 'altogether too commonly used by legal writers in a way which trades on the connotation of the exact and objective measurements of the honest butcher's scales'.[6] Fortunately for the media judicial attitudes are not always homogeneous in this area and Scott J. for example can differentiate between the legal rights of whistleblowers like Peter Wright and the more extensive rights of those repeating the allegations.[7]

On the other side (although the debate does not always have clear polarities) we find assertions that no elaborate balancing of public interests has to be undertaken, and that an absolutist establishmentarian view of communicable information should be conclusive. We find such thinking in for example the rancid rhetoric of Lord Beloff, on a possible 'public interest' defence in the latest Official Secrets Bill debates:

> There is bound to be the odd person who is a self-important nincompoop like Mr Ponting; there is bound to be the muddle-headed young idealist female like Miss Tisdall. They will always be there. What we do not want is to encourage their number to increase by making it seem respectable.[8]

This attitude is embodied particularly in recent legislation such as the Official Secrets Act 1989 and the 'minimalist' Security Service

Act 1989. It has been echoed by prominent members of the judiciary, particularly in the *Spycatcher* case where righteous indignation sometimes produced uncharacteristically forthright statements of political credo. How about this for an attempt to throw a blanket of confidentiality over all disclosure of sensitive information? Lord Donaldson argued in *Spycatcher* in relation to the legal duties of silence owed by Peter Wright and the media respectively that

> the difference may be small because the public interest requirement for secrecy in relation to work which is undertaken for the protection of the realm is of outstanding importance and applies as much to disclosure by newspapers as to disclosure by a member of the service. Indeed it may apply with greater force in the context of a newspaper, because of the extensive nature of the publication. In words well known in the Second World War, 'Careless talk costs lives'.

He concluded that 'the media's right to know and their right to publish is neither more nor less than that of the general public'.[9] This line of reasoning contemplates suppression of all publication and discussion of everything apart from the colour-of-the-carpet-in-the-Ministry-corridor category.

THE *SPYCATCHER* SAGA

This restrictive judicial attitude leads naturally into a general analysis of the *Spycatcher* saga and its aftermath, not in search of elusive doctrinal coherence but in its practical implications for journalists and others. The sad tale of 'bugging and burglary' and other largely unoriginal revelations has yielded as much legal complexity as political embarrassment, and was clearly part of the motivation, along with the Ponting acquittal, for the absolutist lifelong confidentiality drafting of section 1 of the Official Secrets Act 1989, known in parliamentary debates as the 'Spycatcher' clause.

The unavailability of the catch-all section 2 of the Official Secrets Act 1911 against a traitor abroad led to the invocation of the law of confidence as a means of restraint on initial publication and further dissemination of allegations. Unfortunately, widespread publication abroad undermined the force of many arguments for confidentiality but the judiciary were still able to proceed with developing a very malleable area of law, which has its origins in protecting royal etchings[10] and has only relatively recently tackled confidentiality in relation to national security and related matters. As the creature of equity, the law is supposedly independent of statute but it is significant that recently one prominent Law Lord[11] was anxious to align the law as it affects the media with the latest legislative pronouncements on official secrecy, which contain no substantial public interest defences and feeble 'damage' tests, if anything, for the prosecution to satisfy. This view of Lord Templeman subtly trades on constitutional propriety to achieve a version of the law more draconian than would necessarily be reached by autonomous development of confidence law, which has an uncomfortable legacy of public-interest and legitimate-disclosure-of-iniquity criteria available to judges donning their butcher's aprons.

Several strands of legal analysis have to be extricated from the *Spycatcher* saga. First, we have the fate of the pre-trial injunctions aimed at stifling the publication of any *Spycatcher* or related allegations. The UK Courts all in turn upheld the injunctions in 1986 and 1987 despite the widespread publication of *Spycatcher* internationally and its availability in the UK. The European Commission decided that the upholding of the pre-trial injunctions by the House of Lords could not be squared with pressing social need or held to be proportionate to the legitimate aim pursued, since there was a clear need for public debate about the actions of government agents and any possible illegalities involved. The Commission also stressed the fact that employment of the 'private' law of confidence to hamper discussion of information of great public interest correspondingly increased the onus of proof on the government to demonstrate social need. The legal threshold for availability of pre-trial injunctions in this context was merely 'a balance of convenience' test, and this was inadequate.

The judgment of the European Court of Human Rights in November 1991 was however more of a compromise than the Commission's views. The Court distinguished between the initial granting of interlocutory injunctions and their maintenance by the Court of Appeal and the House of Lords after the publication of *Spycatcher* in the United States, and found that the former could be justified in terms of the Convention, but not the latter. The distinction lay in the fact that, once confidentiality had been effectively destroyed, the perpetuation of injunctions would serve a purpose different from the original ostensible one of maintenance of national security and would involve instead the maintenance of security-service morale and the deterrence of other possible traitors.

The argument was that the initial pre-trial injunctions were legitimate because the alternative view could involve the destruction of the basis on which a substantive trial of the merits of the case would be conducted. The outcome is therefore only a small victory for press freedom, since 'gagging' writs have been approved in certain circumstances, and widespread publication elsewhere will not always come to the rescue.

So far as the substantive law of confidence is concerned, the development of the doctrine in the UK has been very restrictive of and hostile to public discussion of sensitive areas. The House of Lords in *Spycatcher* and subsequently have virtually excluded anything other than a lifelong duty of confidentiality for Crown servants in relation to all 'official' information. Exceptionally in *Spycatcher* Lord Brightman did contemplate the theoretical possibility of a service person

> who discovered that some iniquitous course of action was being pursued that was clearly detrimental to our national interest, and he [*sic*] was unable to persuade any senior members of his service or any members of the establishment, or the police, to do anything about it, then he should be relieved of his duty of confidence so that he could alert his fellow citizens to the impending danger.[12]

This restrictiveness in turn creates a poisoned chalice for the media, who succeeded in *Spycatcher* only because of widespread publication in other jurisdictions. The present state of the law is that judicial pronouncements about the legitimate publication of confidential information by third parties are so faltering and evasive that the familiar uncertainties and anxieties remain – in quantifying damage and upholding a case for the public interest in disclosure against the naturally distorted accounts of gravity, etc. given by the executive and endorsed by executive-minded judges.

The civil law of confidence does however in principle contain (for those of the judiciary not so anxious as Lord Templeman to align it with repressive criminal-law criteria) some scope for development of public-interest arguments in favour of publication. Lord Jauncey's recent summary is indicative:

> To what extent a third party receiving information which he [*sic*] knows to be disclosed in breach of confidence will be restrained from publication thereof must depend upon the circumstances. If the information is damaging to national security he will almost certainly be restrained. So far as confidential information which is not

> so damaging is concerned . . . suffice it to say that an agent publishing on behalf of the confidant would probably be constrained . . . as would anyone in the direct chain from the confidant.[13]

So the more indirect and detached dissemination and discussion of sensitive issues (if innocuous to national security) can continue, although the vexed question of determination of damage to national security still rests ultimately with the judiciary.

The third strand in *Spycatcher* is the use of the criminal law of contempt to assist in the process of stifling public debate. Although the law of contempt was supposedly liberalised in the 1981 Contempt of Court Act following the thalidomide affair, the Act expressly left open the application of the criminal law in relation to conduct 'intended to impede or prejudice the administration of justice'.[14] Recently the House of Lords confirmed the view that *The Sunday Times* was in contempt of court for publishing its serialisation of *Spycatcher*, although it had not been named in the original injunctions and the force of these injunctions was notionally unaffected. So a ban on publication by one party effectively bans anyone else. The legal arguments for this extension of liability are not cogent and in the High Court the Vice-Chancellor astutely noted that even if it were a case of the judiciary protecting national security, circuitous enforcement via the law of contempt could not be justified. 'Private rights should not be bolstered by a distortion of the law of contempt in an attempt to produce a judge-made public law protecting official secrets.'[15] Of course disagreement with the trend can be more than merely tactical, as it seems to leave no scope for press freedom. In any event the judiciary were satisfied that this was unexceptionable, as the law clearly established liability, and conventionally if the law is clear, European standards are not applicable. The recent judgment in Strasbourg on the availability of interlocutory injunctions means that this repressive approach can be maintained, at least in the early stages of the operation of the injunctions.

It would appear that there is scant judicial recognition of the purpose and force of the European Convention on Human Rights, and domestic law as it affects the freedom of the press particularly has been fashioned in a concerted manner to achieve goals completely antithetical to the spirit of international obligations. New appointments to the House of Lords could effect some changes, but this is speculative as the tug of precedent is strong and many of the old guard among the judiciary are still around.

OFFICIAL SECRETS – *PLUS ÇA CHANGE*

The climate of pervasive official and institutional secrecy has therefore been gallantly sustained by the judiciary in circumstances where the criminal law has been not directly available. The recent changes in official secrets and related legislation are contributions to this continuity, despite official protestations about liberalisation. The media in some respects were better off and happier with the old law, as will be demonstrated.

The old law

Journalists, as for example in the *ABC* case,[16] have sometimes had section 1 of the 1911 Official Secrets Act and espionage charges to contend with, but the main legal burden on journalists and the media has been section 2, the infamous catch-all section (although its extent has been exaggerated by misrepresentation of the degree to which disclosures can be 'authorised'). Tactically in recent years editors and others have not necessarily been reluctant to work within the confines of discredited and vilified legislation, although they have naturally not broadcast this fact, and may not welcome the supposed transition from blunderbuss to Armalite.

How in practice did the old law impinge on the media? Levels of actual prosecution fluctuated, and 'authorised' histories of intelligence coexisted uneasily with selective prosecution. In terms of day-to-day operation the effect was naturally to limit the amount of official information available because the Act was a complete excuse for non-disclosure, and the mere receipt of information was also an offence, whether or not the information was used. The notion of authorisation embodied in the Act also created great problems. Ministers tended to be self-authorising, senior civil servants tended to leak, and lower echelons were not authorised. So the problems of selective porosity were compounded by those of selective prosecution.

The role of the media in the face of the prosecution of others under the Act should also be noted. The *Tisdall* and *Ponting* cases were classic instances of vindictive prosecutions of civil servants for creating political embarrassment by revealing information unconnected with national security properly-so-called. In the *Tisdall* case the *Guardian* could have been prosecuted under the Official Secrets Act, but it was not. Its tactics will be discussed later, under contempt of court. The *Ponting* case is significant in that the media, through widespread pre-trial publication of the subject matter (the Belgrano sinking), arguably secured his acquittal. In cold legal terms the precedents on the interpretation of the statutory duty to communicate in the interest(s) of the State were not encouraging, as traditionally the judiciary have unsurprisingly had difficulty in separating the interest(s) of the State from those of the government of the day. A 'perverse' jury acquitted Ponting and fuelled opposition to the use of the criminal law where national security and/or corruption were not involved.

The new law

Relations between Government and the media had been soured by the spate of litigation already documented long before the 1989 Act came into force. Official spokespersons for the new legislation maintained in the face of the evidence that it was 'liberalising'; its impact is difficult to assess alongside all the other constraints, and there have been as yet no prosecutions under it.

The only possible peg on which to hang a liberalising label is the identification in the new law of substantive areas, such as security and intelligence, defence, etc. to be protected, as against the catch-all old law. However, prosecutions under the old law all fall within the areas now itemised.

The six categories safeguarded by the Act are security and intelligence, defence, international relations, law and order, information about or obtained by activities under warrants issued under the Interception of Communications Act 1985 and the Security Service Act 1989, and foreign confidences.

The crucial section from the viewpoint of the media is section 5, under which an offence is committed if protected information is disclosed without lawful authority, if the person knows or should know that it is so protected and that it is unauthorised. So far as security and intelligence, defence and international relations are concerned an offence is not committed unless the disclosure is damaging and the person knew or should have known it would be damaging. Surveillance information in section 4 is therefore absolutely protected.

Taken in conjunction with the Security Service Act, which provides no mechanism for proper accountability, the new official secrets law is hardly liberalising. The only other conceivable liberal element in it is that receipt of unauthorised information is no longer an offence *per se*. The most important features of it are the retention of the notion of authorisation, the lack of defences of any substance (at least under the old law a colourable argument could be sustained about the interests of the State) and, for the media in particular, the mere requirement of damage – no element of seriousness or demonstrable threat to national security. Apologists for the legislation have claimed that the 'public interest' is served by the law's requirements, but the law is so weighted against revelation of plots against governments, illegal phone-tapping and other areas of public interest that the narrow establishmentarian sense must be meant.

Ironically, it would appear that while the *Spycatcher* lifelong-confidentiality stipulation in section 1 is exact there is a drafting error in section 5(1) of the Act which, on the face of it, exempts the media in cases of disclosure of protected information by *former* civil servants such as Peter Wright or Antony Cavendish, since the statute refers only to current Crown servants. However, the judiciary has loyally plugged the gap (Lord Templeman on this occasion breaking with constitutional propriety) by simply asserting that the section does not mean what it says.[17]

If we bear in mind the shibboleth that it is not just the Official Secrets Act itself which is the problem, illiberal though it is, but official secrecy in general, then the new law has to be assessed in conjunction with other constraints such as tighter disciplinary codes for civil servants, contractual undertakings not to publish unvetted memoirs, and the D-Notice system. The relationship between the D-Notice system and the new law requires further exposition.[18]

It is well known that only the British would describe the informal network of D-Notice constraints as a voluntary system. Its avowed purpose is to protect information particularly sensitive in national security terms, and editors have frequent recourse to the Secretary of the Committee.

The latest categories protected under the 1989 Act correlate quite closely with D-Notice categories, although their scope is not identical. Under the old law there was no defence involving assessment of damage, whereas under the 1989 Act knowledge or reasonable cause to know that disclosure is damaging is relevant. Therefore evidence about non-committal advice from the Secretary could well be admissible when culpability is assessed by the jury in a criminal case or indeed by the judge in a breach of confidence action.

In essence therefore the new law further reduces the chances of informed debate about vast areas of legitimate public concern, although there is the optimistic and as yet unfounded argument that absolutist legislation of this type will be counterproductive and generate leaks. Advocates of the new law have been essentially reduced to two tactics, one of scaremongering and exaggerating the risks involved in ventilation of certain issues, the other of misrepresentation of the severity of the law, when clearly it has gaps where prior-publication or public-interest defences should be. Section 2 of the 1911 Act was under a cloud for over twenty years, but in some respects the remedy is worse than the disease. Quite apart from its practical impact, its symbolic denunciatory aspect provides powerful ideological reinforcement. It must also be assessed in a context where internal disciplinary codes for civil servants have been tightened up. Finally it should not be forgotten that section 1 of the old law, dealing with espionage, survives.

CONTEMPT OF COURT AND PROTECTION OF SOURCES

Another related area of legal constraint is concerned with the protection of sources of information, crucial to many journalistic activities. The Contempt of Court Act 1981 section 10 decreed that courts could not require the disclosure of a source or sources of information unless satisfied that such disclosure was necessary either in the interest of justice, or of national security, or for the prevention of disorder or crime. However, this provision has not protected journalists as much as a straightforward reading might suggest.

In the *Tisdall* case the court held that the *Guardian* should surrender a leaked Ministry of Defence memo, not because of any intrinsic danger to national security but simply to prevent further, more serious disclosures! Subsequent cases in the commercial sphere such as *Warner*[19] and *Goodwin*[20] have revealed an equally hostile judicial attitude to the putative statutory protection. So in the absence of legal protection journalists intent on protecting sources rather better than the *Guardian* did would be well advised to destroy the material in question.

CONCLUSION

Griffith pessimistically concludes his analysis of official secrets legislation with observation of the 'apparent reluctance of those with authority in the press and broadcasting to fight for the freedoms entrusted to them'.[21] He could have added that the ammunition with which to fight is being increasingly and systematically withheld even from those with the stomach for it.

How should journalists and the media operate in the face of all the restrictions documented? The problems are so pervasive that advice is difficult. Such actions as withdrawing from the official press lobby system keep ideological garments clean but achieve little else. Larger-scale opposition is hard to generate. The most ringing declarations in support of press freedom currently come from Brussels and Strasbourg (although the latest pronouncement from the European Court is more muted) and will take time to be grudgingly reflected in the UK law, at which point they will again become vulnerable to an unsympathetic judiciary.

How would it be possible to change the prevailing political culture, the 'British disease' of secrecy? An incoming Labour government was committed to introducing Freedom of Information legislation to attempt sensibly to demarcate the inaccessible and the accessible. Such legislation is fraught with possible pitfalls, since establishment of, say, public access to official documents held by government would be hedged about with exceptions and exemptions, and activities like weeding of files are difficult to proscribe effectively. The ideal would presumably be to guarantee rights to information without involving ministerial or civil service or judicial discretion.

If any legislation followed the pattern of David Steel's unsuccessful Freedom of Information Bill (No. 2) of 1984 it might however at least stipulate that protection of specified classes of information be dependent on demonstration of risk of serious harm through disclosure, thereby partially liberalising the already 'liberalised' 1989 Official Secrets Act. But that achievement would be largely negative.

It is difficult to pin hopes on Bills of Rights, Citizens Charters or other constitutional entrenchments of basic political freedoms. The recent American experience of steady erosion of established Freedom of Information entitlements, especially where national security is allegedly at stake, does not inspire confidence.[22]

So for the foreseeable future the snaffle and the curb are likely to be more prominent than the horse.[23]

NOTES

1 Roy Campbell, 'On Some South African Novelists' *Collected Poems* (London, The Bodley Head, 1960). In this context the horse could be press freedom.
2 Innocuous radio programmes such as *My Country Right or Wrong* came under fire, as did other publications. (*My Country Right or Wrong*, BBC Radio 4, 28, 29 and 30 June 1988. Previously banned by injunction.)
3 *R* v. *Ponting* [1985] Crim LR 318.
4 Hansard, House of Commons, 147 *H.C. Debs*, col. 1082 (22 February 1989).
5 *Attorney General* v. *The Observer Ltd and Others* and *Attorney General* v. *Times Newspaper Ltd and Another*, both in *Times Law Report* 22 December 1987.
6 D.N. MacCormick, *Legal Reasoning and Legal Theory* (Oxford, Clarendon Press, 1978), p. 112.
7 See note 5.
8 Hansard, House of Lords, 505 *H.L. Debs*, col. 922 (3 April 1989).
9 [1988] 2 WLR 873–4.
10 *Prince Albert* v. *Strange* (1849) 1 Mac and G 25.
11 Lord Templeman in *Lord Advocate* v. *The Scotsman*, [1989] 3 WLR 366.
12 [1988] 3 WLR 795.
13 [1989] 3 WLR 370–1.
14 Contempt of Court Act 1981, s.6(c).
15 [1987] 3 All ER 289 a.
16 *R* v. *Aubrey, Berry and Campbell* (1978). They were convicted under s.2, but charges under s.1 were dropped.
17 [1989] 3 WLR 368.
18 See further on this D. Fairley, 'D Notices, Official Secrets and the Law', *Oxford Journal of Legal Studies*, 10 (1990), pp. 430–40.
19 *In re* An Inquiry under the Company Securities (Insider Dealing) Act 1985, [1988] AC 660.
20 *X Ltd* v. *Morgan Grampian Plc* [1990] 2 WLR 100.
21 J. Griffith, 'The Official Secrets Act', *Journal of Law and Society*, 16 (1989), pp. 273–90.
22 R.O. Currey (ed.), *Freedom at Risk: Secrecy, Censorship and Repression in the 1980s* (Philadelphia, Temple University Press, 1988).
23 See note 1, above.

Chapter 5

Codes of conduct for journalists

Nigel G.E. Harris

Codes of conduct are in fashion. In Britain more that 350 occupational organisations have their own codes, and the numbers are increasing each year. A similar situation obtains in several other countries, including the United States. Journalism was one of the first professions to have such codes, and it is still a source of new ones.

One of the most noteworthy features of codes for journalists is just how wide is the range of countries in which they have been adopted. They are found not just in western Europe and North America, but in countries as diverse as Egypt, South Korea, Jamaica, Mali and Venezuela.[1] Most are fairly brief documents that could be expressed in no more than a dozen or so sentences, though in common with the practice in other professions there is now a tendency to draw up longer codes – a good example from Britain is that recommended in the Calcutt Report,[2] an amended version of which has been adopted by the Press Complaints Commission.

If a country has one or more codes of conduct for journalists, their general purpose will have been determined to a great extent by the systems of regulation in that country. Where journalistic malpractice of most kinds is illegal, and where there is little scope for self-regulation by the profession, there will be little point in drafting a code which exhorts reporters and editors to avoid such malpractice. Under repressive regimes a code may be a way of giving moral support to journalists who have been victimised, and of encouraging solidarity within the profession. Under more liberal regimes codes will place greater emphasis on protecting members of the public rather than journalists themselves.

The sorts of contents a code has will depend on the kind of body that drew it up. In Britain codes have been produced by a trade union (the National Union of Journalists), a publishers association (the Newspaper Publishers Association), a government appointed committee (the Calcutt Committee), and a statutory body (the Broadcasting Standards Council); the United States has examples of ones produced by newspaper editors (the American Society of Newspaper Editors) and radio and television news directors (Radio/Television News Directors Association). The interests of members of a journalism trade union will not always be identical with those of the publishers of a newspaper that employs them. It would be surprising if we were to find any code drawn up by newspaper publishers which contained a clause asserting a right of journalists to have their opinions printed when these were quite contrary to the convictions of the publishers, but there would be nothing odd about finding such a clause in a code drafted by a journalism trade union.

PRESS CODES AND BROADCASTING CODES

The greater proportion of codes of conduct for journalists have to do with reporting for the press, rather than for news broadcasts. One reason for this is the relatively recent growth in the numbers and length of news programmes on radio and television; another is the fact that in most developed countries there is much greater government control over broadcasting than over the press. Where there are separate codes for broadcast journalism, it is not surprising that these should be found in countries, such as the United States[3] and Canada,[4] which have a heavy concentration of commercial broadcasting outlets. In Australia the code of the Australian Journalists' Association, which was drawn up originally with the needs of the press and its readers in mind, has now been revised so that its clauses are applicable both to journalists working for newspapers and to those employed in the electronic media.[5] In Britain the Code of Practice of the Broadcasting Standards Council is concerned with the whole range of broadcast programmes, but includes some substantial sections on news broadcasts. However, its guidance is directed at news-room editors rather than at reporters and cameramen in the field, although the latter will, of course, be affected by the Council's influence on editorial policy.

There is little difference between the codes written explicitly for broadcast journalists and those for press journalists in the kinds of action they list as prohibited. This is not surprising, since until fairly recently the problems about the quality of news material, and the means by which it is acquired, have been similar for both types of media. Broadcast journalism was originally modelled very closely on press journalism, but things are changing. The division between television and radio news broadcasts and current affairs discussion programmes is becoming ever more blurred; the anchorperson has become an interviewer of world figures, a chair of debates and even a negotiator; and with CNN coverage of the Gulf War we have entered an age not only of all-day news programmes, but, more importantly, of *live* news as that which is given the highest priority. All this makes the nature of broadcast news diverge more and more from that found in newspapers, yet so far the relevant codes of conduct have been left behind and most have nothing to say about the new ethical issues that these trends are producing. For instance, no guidance is given about how to respond when incidents are staged for the cameras. This was already a limited problem for photojournalism, though not one addressed in the press codes, but it is a much more serious one for live television coverage.

It is to the credit of the Broadcasting Standards Council that in its code it *has* addressed some of the ethical problems which are more pressing for television news-editors than for their press counterparts. It pays particular attention to the showing of scenes of violence on television, since these are likely to have a far more marked effect on viewers than would still pictures of the same events published in the press. The code suggests various factors that should be considered when deciding how much violence it is appropriate to show in a news broadcast, but it also points to a number of less widely recognised problems such as the fact that repeated showings of the same scene of violence in successive news broadcasts could 'breed indifference or revulsion'. The code also deals more briefly (in so far as news broadcasts are concerned) with items that involve reference to sexual behaviour or which raise questions of taste and decency, such as ones in which bad language is used. Because none of the other broadcasting codes address the issues peculiar to broadcasting, I shall not single them out for any special attention in the following discussion.

Although newspapers carry a great deal of material that is not news, it is merely those parts of them that do convey news, and that involve the work of reporters, which are currently the subject of press codes of conduct. The quality of some other kinds of newspaper material may, however, be considered to be a matter of editorial responsibility and thus an appropriate subject for codified guidance. One area of newspaper practice that has been singled out for codification is advertising,[6] but there are others where as yet no codes give guidance.

Take, as an example, the wide variety of advice columns carried in many papers, ranging over health, personal relationships, gardening, travel and financial matters. Some are written by professional journalists, but others are obtained from 'expert' contributors. Two of the major British codes[7] make reference to the special dangers of giving financial advice self-interestedly, but otherwise advice giving is something that is ignored. Yet editors should surely be seen as taking responsibility for ensuring that the person giving the advice is appropriately qualified. Where advice is on specialist matters which could affect people's well-being, press codes could require conformity to the practices of giving the status of the advice provider and recommending readers to obtain an independent professional opinion before acting on the advice.[8]

THE REGULATORY FRAMEWORK

Codes of conduct are only a part, and perhaps a quite minor part, of the regulatory framework within which journalists operate. Reporters and editors may be constrained in many different ways from acting unethically. For their own job security it will be prudent for journalists to avoid acting in ways to which their proprietors might object; and because most newspapers rely so heavily on revenue from advertising, they will be under pressure not to offend major advertisers or, indeed, their readers, since a drop in circulation will lead to a reduction in advertising revenue. In adjudicating on complaints, regulatory bodies such as press councils may rely not merely on interpreting codes of conduct, but on their own judgement as to what should or should not be deemed to be acceptable; so journalists whose work lies within the jurisdiction of such a body, and who wish to avoid having complaints made and upheld against them will need to take note of its decisions and the reasons given for those decisions.

One especially important constraining factor can be the law. Some kinds of invasion of privacy such as telephone-tapping may be criminal offences; so too may be certain actions that are contrary to the public interest such as the disclosure of secrets about the defence of the realm. Other actions could lead to costly lawsuits with hefty damages being awarded against the journalists or their newspapers –

libel provides the most obvious example of this – and this may discourage editors from carrying material which could lead to their being faced with legal action. While it is probably true that in the majority of cases what would be illegal would also be unethical, in some cases journalists may be discouraged from pursuing an ethically correct form of action for fear of the legal consequences: occasionally, for instance, the public interest is served by the leaking of state secrets. Again, it could be unfortunate if a journalist were to refrain from giving a frank appraisal of someone's suitability for public office for fear of the action for libel. One of the reasons for seeking not to have *statutory* codes of conduct for journalists is that they are likely to increase the range of situations in which reporters or editors are faced with a dilemma between acting legally and acting ethically.

WHOM DOES A CODE BENEFIT?

It is members of the public who are most usually identified as benefiting from the existence of codes of conduct. Indeed, when ordinary people have suffered at the hands of unscrupulous professionals, there is often a demand that the profession concerned should draw up a code of conduct, or strengthen an existing code, so as to outlaw such behaviour. It should be remembered, however, that the existence of a code is not in itself a guarantee of greater protection, for its requirements may be ignored; if so, then, far from protecting them, the list of fine-sounding clauses that make up a code may lull a credulous public into placing its trust in members of the profession to an extent that is quite unwarranted.

If a code offers public protection it will not be the public in general which gains directly, but rather particular individuals or sections of the public with whom members of the profession have some kind of relationship. With codes for journalists there are three types of direct beneficiary. First, there are readers of the newspaper or periodical for which the journalist works. Clauses which lay down the requirement that reports should be truthful, accurate, objective etc., can be seen as designed to protect readers from being manipulated and to allow them to rely on the information given in those reports when making their daily decisions. Second, there are individuals from whom the journalist obtains material. For example, a code may state that a journalist should not breach the confidence of a source who has given information only on condition that his or her identity not be disclosed. And third, there are those whose story a journalist is investigating. Thus, a code may also state that a reporter should not harrass or intrude on the privacy of the person or persons about whom he or she is writing.

Although a code may benefit directly only those who have a relationship with the journalist to which it applies, the public at large could gain indirectly from the code's existence. If the having of the code leads to a higher standard of journalism, then this could encourage even those not covered by it into adopting better ethical practices, since in any walk of life people adhere by and large to what is the going ethical standard in behaviour among their friends and colleagues. It may also benefit the profession itself, by enhancing public respect for it and giving its members more reason to place confidence in each other's integrity.

The trend towards the introduction of longer codes carries some dangers with it. It might seem that when a code contains detailed specifications of what is deemed to be unethical, rather than having just a few rather vague general principles, this will increase the extent to which the code can offer protection to the public. However, one of the consequences of bringing out detailed sets of regulations is that it fosters a loophole-seeking attitude of mind. The result could be that journalists will come to treat as permissible anything that does not fit the precise specifications of unethical behaviour. Furthermore, short codes consisting of a few broad principles can often be applied to new types of situation which could not have been envisaged by those drawing them up; detailed sets of guidelines, on the other hand, may need to be amended with changing circumstances, and since the revision of codes is a time-consuming task, anomalies may not be rectified in the short term.

ENFORCEMENT OF CODES

It is the limited powers that most professional bodies have to enforce their codes which throws into question the public benefits of having codes of conduct, at least of the non-statutory kind. If breaches go unpunished, if complaints produce no more than verbal criticisms from the body that deals with them and these are then ignored by those against whom they are made, then what protection will the public gain from the existence of the code? Of course, the code may reinforce the behaviour of those who are naturally wont to adhere to high professional standards, but they will be ineffective in controlling mavericks.

In only a few professions, such as medicine and the law, do professional bodies have the power to enforce their codes of conduct by being able, as an ultimate sanction, to prevent those who are in serious breach of the codes from carrying on working as members of the profession. In those professions it is possible to do this, because registration as a member of the professional association is a statutory requirement for being employed in them.

Should we then press for a similar registration scheme for journalists as the way to solve the problem of maverick reporters who blatantly ignore the principles enshrined in a code of conduct applicable to them? I think not. Such a scheme, if applied in the case of journalism, would raise dangers which are not present with professions like medicine. In the vast majority of cases where doctors act unethically and are disciplined, there is no political dimension to their actual or supposed wrongdoing. With journalism there are certainly some actions where what is generally condemned has nothing whatever to do with political matters, for example, intrusions into the privacy of film stars. But many investigative journalists, if they are to obtain material for their stories, have to come close to acting in breach of their professional codes of conduct, particularly when dealing with corruption or mismanagement in government agencies. Most codes have a let-out clause allowing the obtaining of information by what would otherwise be questionable means, when the publication of that information is in the public interest. The danger of having a registration scheme for journalists is that it is not inconceivable that those who administered such a scheme might come to have pressure put on them to strike off particular journalists, by the very politicians or bureaucrats whose actions those reporters are investigating, and that on occasion they might accede to that pressure.

TYPES OF CLAUSE CONTAINED IN CODES

A code of conduct for journalists may contain clauses of a kind which are relevant to many professions. This is obviously true of those which exhort members of the profession to refrain from acting in a manner which would bring the profession into disrepute, but it is also true of some other types of clause. There are, for instance, codes for journalists and for lawyers which demand that members of the profession should act in their private lives in ways which do not produce conflicts of interest with their professional duties.[9] Again, both journalists and foresters have been required in their respective codes to act fairly in their dealings with other members of their profession.[10] However, the vast majority of clauses found in codes of conduct for journalists are appropriate only for those engaged in that profession or in closely related occupations.

I have already identified various groups of people whose interests may be protected by a code. On the whole most clauses that appear in codes can be seen as being of primary benefit to one specific category of person, while, perhaps, being of some consequential benefit to others. In discussing the various types of stipulation found in codes it will be convenient to treat in turn the clauses which benefit those different groups. Although this is a useful and, perhaps, revealing way of approaching the codes, it should be noted that none of the existing codes for journalists explicitly lists it clauses in this way.[11] In the space available it will be possible to describe only a selection of the more important or more interesting matters which are dealt with in major codes from around the world.

READERS' INTERESTS

Many people read newspapers or watch television news as a form of entertainment – the feelings involved can vary from vicarious joy to *schadenfreude*, from nail-biting suspense to mildly satisfied curiosity – but however strong is any pleasure-seeking motive in readers or viewers, they still expect some reliability in the information presented to them.[12] Thus, codes for journalists commonly require reporters to convey only material possessing certain of the attributes which help to ensure reliability. Reporters may be required to give the truth; to write accurately and objectively; to avoid distortion, selection or misrepresentation of the facts; to avoid bias and partiality; to refrain from conjecture or the passing off of opinion as fact.

Sometimes these requirements may be breached through carelessness or laziness; sometimes through an over-zealousness in seeking to make a scoop, as may happen when there is a temptation to treat some likely happening, such as a ministerial resignation, as having already occurred. There are, however, cases which seem to merit much greater moral condemnation than these, ones in which what is reported is deliberately distorted, or in which material facts are deliberately suppressed, so as to fit in with the interests of a third party, perhaps a key advertiser or someone who has given benefits directly to the journalist concerned. Since the distortion or suppression will be carried out in the interests of the third party, and since that party will normally have a motive for bringing about those distortions or suppressions only when they are against the interests of readers or viewers, the journalist involved can be seen as involved in a cynical manipulation of the public. Readers who find themselves to have been used in this way are likely to feel, and have good reason to feel, aggrieved; the journalist responsible will have seriously compromised the trust they have placed in him or her. Thus, it is not surprising that most codes include clauses explicitly condemning the acceptance of bribes or other inducements. Codes drawn up by journalists themselves (such as that of the National Union of Journalists) may also exhort reporters not to allow themselves to be influenced in what they report by commercial pressures such as fear of offending advertisers; this sort of clause is not found in the codes drawn up by newspaper proprietors. While having a clause advocating that journalists should resist allowing commercial considerations to influence their reporting is most clearly in the interests of newspaper readers, it can also be in the interests of journalists themselves. Good journalists, as with the better people in any profession, pride themselves on their integrity, and they will find it easier to maintain that integrity against pressure brought by less scrupulous proprietors if they can point to a clause in their professional code which supports them in making a stand against their being used in this way.

SOURCES

Many of those who provide information for reporters are quite happy to be identified publicly, for example, if they are acting as official spokespersons or if they happen to be chance witnesses to some disaster. There are others, however, who are willing to talk only on condition that their identity is kept secret. Such requests for confidentiality may, for instance, come from those who wish to expose some kind of corruption occurring in the organisation for which they work. If their identity is not kept secret, they could lose their employment and, in extreme cases, their lives could be put at risk. Most codes for journalists therefore include a clause requiring them to honour any undertakings they have made to sources to keep their identities confidential.

Although the adherence by journalists to this rule is most obviously of importance to the sources concerned, it also benefits journalists themselves. If reporters took to disclosing the identities of even a small proportion of their confidential sources, then it is likely that such sources would dry up; for who would risk becoming such a source, unless they could feel considerable confidence that their anonymity would be preserved? This is one reason why journalists have been prepared to be found guilty of contempt of court rather than disclose the identity of a source when ordered to do so by a judge in open court.

A more contentious matter is where sources demand confidentiality, not about their identity, but about some of the information provided by them. This is less clearly covered by the main British and US codes which all talk of 'protecting confidential sources', but in the Australian Journalists' Association code the requirement is to 'respect all confidences received in the cause of their calling'.[13] Politicians sometimes give reporters minor information 'on the record', and then demand an undertaking that the rest of what they say should be treated as 'off the record', i.e., confidentially. Having received such a promise they may then disclose particularly newsworthy information, which they know the journalists will feel duty-bound to refrain from publishing. Reporters need to guard against being manipulated thus; but it could be argued that where a politician is trying deliberately to hamstring journalists in this way, their trust is being abused, thereby negating the force of their undertaking to the politician.

PERSONS IN THE NEWS

There are two kinds of action which may cause distress or other harm to those who are the potential subject of news stories. These are, first, the actions taken in obtaining the news material and, second, the publishing of that material.

Some of the more recently drafted codes[14] have clauses that explicitly require journalists not to intrude on personal privacy. These have been incorporated because of public outrage at the gross intrusions into privacy involved in cases such as that which occurred in 1990, when Gorden Kaye, a television actor who had suffered serious head injuries in a freak accident, was photographed by an employee of the *Sunday Sport* in a private room in hospital, despite a notice on the door asking all visitors to contact a member of staff before entering. Indeed, largely as a result of that case, the Press Complaints Commission code has a clause requiring 'journalists or photographers making enquiries at hospitals or similar institutions' to 'identify themselves to a responsible official and obtain permission before entering non-public areas'.

In the Gorden Kaye case the journalist and photographer who entered his hospital room did not resort to any kind of deception. They did not, for instance, masquerade as doctors or pretend that they were friends of the patient. However, reporters have sometimes resorted to impersonation or otherwise hiding their identity when obtaining a story. A number of codes rule against journalists using misrepresentation or subterfuge when seeking to obtain information. Such clauses obviously ban actions in which positive steps are taken to deceive, but it is not clear that they cover cases of deception by default, where an interviewee is deceived because he or she mistakenly presumes that the person asking them questions is someone other than a journalist, such as, say, a market researcher or some distant acquaintance. Such passive deceit is banned by a clause in the Australian Journalists' Association code, which requires that reporters 'shall identify themselves and their employers before obtaining any interview for publication or broadcast'.[15]

If, despite requesting to be left alone, a person in the news is accosted persistently by a journalist asking for a statement, or if someone's house is 'staked out' by a pack of reporters or photographers, this may constitute harassment. Although the former sort of case is dealt with in some codes of conduct, it is hard to see how a code addressed to *individual* journalists could cover the latter adequately; for sometimes what may be found objectionable is not the mere presence of journalists, but there being a sizeable crowd of them waiting around.

I turn now to clauses which are designed to offer protection to people in respect of what is published about them. There are several matters that may be covered in these.

First, there are clauses which require those who have been treated, in their view at least, unfairly, to be given an opportunity to reply. If such a clause is to be included in a code, it is important that it should say that replies should be given a prominence similar to that given to the original stories. Even this may seem too little, since the damage caused by a story may not be offset adequately by the publication of a reply, but it is hard to see how a code could require more.

Second, there are clauses which list various types of information which editors should refrain from publishing. Examples are the giving of the identity of rape victims where (for example, in the United States) it is legal to do so, and the identifying of innocent relatives or friends of those convicted of crimes.

A third type of clause is that which condemns the use of discriminatory language, for example, in drawing attention to details of a person's race, colour, religion, sex or sexual orientation, when these are not directly relevant to the story being covered.

PROTECTING JOURNALISTS THEMSELVES

I have argued that many of the clauses which are designed prima facie to protect members of some group of persons other than journalists, can also be seen as helpful to those journalists who try to maintain high standards in their own work and who wish to encourage others to do likewise. I have also mentioned that in countries where reporters and editors can suffer persecution, codes of conduct may be used to encourage feelings of solidarity. Thus, for example, in the code of the Venezuelan Association of Journalists is found a clause which requires that: 'The journalist should give his support to his colleagues when they are being unjustly persecuted or are victims of acts violating the established law or from all other forms of provoked repression.'[16]

In countries where journalists are in relatively little danger of suffering such persecution, clauses designed to protect journalists themselves are rare or non-existent. One matter which is covered in very few codes is plagiarism,[17] yet I agree with Conrad Fink when he writes:

> If ever a rule was part of the journalistic fabric, it is that a reporter should not steal or rewrite another reporter's story. Written codes of ethics don't spell that out. Perhaps they must in the future, particularly because news work can create conditions where reporters unthinkingly can commit plagiarism.[18]

One reason why hardly any existing codes include such a clause is that plagiarism has not become a topic of public debate. When codes of conduct are drawn up, those who draft them seldom aim to give comprehensive guidance on the full range of ethical decisions that may face those working in the profession; normally, they confine their attention to matters dealt with in previous codes, plus any new issue that is a current source of public disquiet.

CHEQUE-BOOK JOURNALISM

All the types of clause found in codes which I have discussed above are ones designed to protect persons or groups of persons from harm which they do not deserve to suffer. But it is also possible to have clauses which are designed to prevent benefits accruing to the undeserving. An example from the Press Complaints Commission code is a clause which recommends that payment should not be made 'for stories, pictures or information . . . to people engaged in crime or their associates except where the material concerned ought to be published in the public interest and the payment is necessary for this to be done'.

For people actually to profit as a result of having committed serious crimes, by being paid large sums of money for their stories, is something many members of the public find particularly obnoxious. Yet why confine the ban to just these cases? There are good reasons for holding that cheque-book journalism is undesirable even where those who benefit from the payments have neither committed a crime, nor are associated in any way with criminals. Payments to ex-spouses or ex-employees of public figures for 'revelations' about the private lives of their former marriage partners or bosses, provide an example. There is something rather distasteful about such sources gaining financially from disclosing the personal secrets of others. There is also a risk that those who are paid in this manner will resort to exaggeration in order to reap the highest rewards. I think, therefore, it would be reasonable to criticise the existing codes for not condemning cheque-book journalism more broadly.

However, this issue brings me on to a further point, which is that serious limitations are placed on the scope of codes for journalists by the moral standards – the actual rather than the purported ones – of the public themselves. It may be particularly wrong for people to break confidences about other's private lives and be paid for doing so, but it is hardly an admirable spectacle when people provide the press with such stories, not for money but out of spite. Even though some of us may think there is something undesirable about such stories being published, we could hardly expect a code of conduct to try to outlaw their publication. To a considerable extent newspapers have to provide the public with what it wants; and if a large proportion of the population is especially attracted to buy newspapers when they carry salacious material, then editors of papers that are marketed to those people cannot afford to take a high moral stance and refuse to print anything of this kind. Of course, there is no need for them to give in entirely to public demands. Many journalists, who are unhappy about pandering to readers' tastes, no doubt choose to try to educate them into having broader interests, especially about matters of legitimate public concern, such as environmental issues or social problems; but, usually, it is the kind of journalists who will not be so motivated that the drafters of codes are planning to influence.

A code which merely advocated ideal standards of behaviour for journalists, and made no link between those standards and what people actually do, would be considered irrelevant by most practising journalists, and hence would be unlikely to influence their actions. If a code is to be effective in bringing about improvements in the professional behaviour of reporters and editors, it is more likely to be successful if it starts from the basis of actual practice. Nevertheless, many existing codes, particularly those in Britain, seem unnecessarily negative in tone: they present lists of the types of action which are to be avoided, but say relatively little about what would constitute *good* practice and how it might be achieved.

NOTES

1 For details of these and many other codes see J.C. Jones, *Mass Media Codes of Ethics and Councils: A Comparative International Study on Professional Standards* (Paris, Unesco, 1980). Some of those reproduced in that work have now been revised. Codes of conduct are usually not expressly published, but are issued to members of the organisation concerned, and to other interested parties on request. Where they have been reproduced in published works I shall give the appropriate reference, but where I give no reference I know of no *published* source.

2 Home Office, *Report of the Committee on Privacy and Related Matters* (London, HMSO, 1990), pp. 121–4.

3 The Code of Broadcast News Ethics of the Radio/Television News Directors Association, reproduced in C. Fink, *Media Ethics: In the Newsroom and Beyond* (New York, McGraw-Hill, 1988), pp. 293–5.

4 The code of the Radio/Television News Directors Association of Canada is similar to that of its US counterpart.

5 See L. Apps, 'Media Ethics in Australia', *Journal of Mass Media Ethics*, 5 (1990), pp. 117–35.

6 In Britain the relevant code is the extremely detailed British Code of Advertising Practice issued by the Code of Advertising Practice Committee; in contrast, the Advertising Code of American Business, drafted by the American Advertising Federation and the Association of Better Business Bureaus International, consists of only ten sentences. The latter is reproduced in Fink, op. cit., p. 303.

7 Those of the Press Complaints Commission and of the Institute of Journalists. The latter is reproduced in N.G.E. Harris, *Professional Codes of Conduct in The United Kingdom: A Directory* (London, Mansell, 1989), pp. 179–80.
8 The Independent Committee for the Supervision of Standards of Telephone Information Services includes just such a clause in *its* Code of Practice.
9 The Society of Professional Journalists (in the United States – see Fink, op.cit., p. 290) and the Faculty of Advocates (in Scotland).
10 The Australian Journalists' Association code in force from 1944 to 1984 (see Apps, op. cit., p. 118) – surprisingly, this clause was dropped when the code was revised – and, in the United Kingdom, the Institute of Chartered Foresters (Harris, op. cit., p. 169).
11 It is rare in the codes of other professions too (that of the British Institute of Management being a noteworthy exception – see Harris, op. cit., pp. 96–9).
12 A somewhat controversial exception is provided by publications like the *Sunday Sport*, which are published with a newspaper's format, but in which the stories about bizarre sexual practices, sightings of extra-terrestrial beings etc., are such that only the most credulous of readers could have much faith in their factual accuracy.
13 Apps, op. cit., p. 122.
14 For example, the revised code of the Australian Journalists' Association, and, in Britain, that of the Press Complaints Commission.
15 Apps, op. cit., p. 123.
16 Jones, op. cit., p. 42.
17 One (rather obscure) code which does refer to plagiarism is the Declaration of Rights and Obligations of Journalists that was approved by the journalists' unions of the European Community (as it then existed) in 1971. See Jones, op. cit., p. 76.
18 Fink, op. cit., p. 98.

Chapter 6

Privacy, publicity and politics

Andrew Belsey

Privacy and alleged invasions of privacy by the media are central issues in the ethics of journalism. Clearly, we live in a society that values personal privacy, and is concerned about intrusions into privacy from whatever source, including the media. Yet, perhaps paradoxically, we also live in a society that thrives on publicity, or at least one in which many individuals depend on publicity for their lives and activities.[1]

This seeming paradox is usually defused by drawing a distinction between the private and the public aspects of people's lives, and by further claiming that there is indeed a right to privacy, but that in certain circumstances the right can be overridden in the name of 'the public interest'. This account of the matter accepts that in such circumstances an invasion of privacy has actually occurred but that the invasion can be justified by an appeal to a greater good.

I shall dispute this account and argue instead that the right to privacy is no more than a presumption (though an important one), and that where some information about an individual that he or she would prefer to keep private *should* be in the public domain, then putting it there is not overriding that individual's right to privacy because no such right ever existed concerning this aspect of the person's life. There is, on this account, no such thing as a justifiable invasion of privacy because justification is in fact a demonstration that no privacy could properly be claimed in the first place. On this account, all invasions of privacy are unjustifiable.

This is particularly important in the case of politicians and others who occupy similar positions in society. Thus a politician who has his or her 'secret love nest' exposed in the press is not the victim of an invasion of privacy, because scandalous behaviour of this nature cannot legitimately claim the protection of privacy. This is not simply because politicians are in the public eye, but because they, and others in business and the media as well, wield power in society, and all aspects of the exercise of power must be open to public scrutiny. This is the only way to avoid corruption in public life, and by corruption I mean more than financial chicanery. I do not say that politicians are not entitled to privacy, but that they are not entitled to abuse the right to privacy. In a democracy those who wield power cannot decide for themselves where to draw the boundary between the public and the private aspects of their lives.

I shall argue this case from the position in moral theory that what should be done is what is best, overall, for everyone whose interests are involved. Having arrived at what is best, it is then perfectly proper to talk about rights as a way of indicating the protection due to individuals and their interests. There is a right to privacy because it is better to live in a society in which privacy is respected and protected. Perhaps it would be possible to go further and claim that it would be intolerable to live in a society in which privacy was constantly abused or non-existent. However, precisely because we live in a society, there are limits to privacy. When that society is based on a democratic but non-egalitarian distribution of power and privilege, then there are further limits to privacy, in the sense that the lives of those who exercise power should be above suspicion, which means that they must be open to scrutiny.

PRIVACY AND PUBLICITY IN MODERN SOCIETY

Privacy is regarded as valuable, and I shall accept that it is valuable. Its value is recognised by its being entrenched in international codes and conventions. Thus Article 12 of the Universal Declaration of Human Rights stated as long ago as 1948 that

> No one shall be subjected to arbitrary interference with his [*sic*] privacy, family, home or correspondence, nor to attacks upon his [*sic*] honour and reputation. Everyone has the right to the protection of the law against such interference or attacks.

The protection offered to privacy by this Article has in recent years been called upon in three (overlapping) areas where individual rights have come under threat:

1 Surveillance by private or (more likely) state security organisations, including the compiling of secret dossiers on people

through the use of illegal or illegitimate methods such as phone-tapping, bugging, etc.

2 Unauthorised access to private or confidential data, often held in computer files, such as financial and tax affairs, social-security status, medical records, criminal records, etc.
3 Invasions of privacy by the press, first, by the physical intrusion of reporters into someone's personal life and private space, and second, by the splashing of that person's name, picture and story across screens or the pages of the tabloids, often with the utmost insensitivity or vulgarity.

In spite of the recent introduction in the UK of some legislative safeguards in the first two areas, there is little that members of the public can do to assure themselves that their privacy is not being abused here. They simply do not know what is going on and cannot find out, for such abuse is normally hidden at source, even though it might have actual consequences for people's lives. With invasions of privacy by the press it is wholly different, for here the victim obviously knows. This might explain why there is a considerable outcry against invasions of privacy by the press – even though this is less harmful to individuals and the democratic political process than abuses in the other two areas – for here is an open target, easily identifiable, to soak up the public's concern and wrath.

Hence the demand for the press to 'clean up its act', either voluntarily or, if this fails, through controls imposed by legislation. This threat of statutory restraints prompted the editors of the national newspapers in Britain to issue their own Code of Practice in 1989 to add to codes promulgated by bodies such as the Press Council (now defunct) and the National Union of Journalists. The editors' code and the Press Council code were later absorbed into a newpaper-industry code, monitored by the Press Complaints Commission, in which the voluntary protection of privacy, without legislative intervention, was a primary aim.

And yet strangely, the same public that can get so heated about invasions of privacy by the press is willing to lap up the results by buying the offending papers in large quantities (though in 1991 circulations were falling). The justification offered by the press for its activities – that it is only giving the public what it wants – is not without foundation. But there is more to it than this. The actual role of the press is not just to entertain its readers but to focus willingly accepted publicity on people who require it and desire it, people in the public eye who want to stay there, and people not yet in the public eye who want to get there.

So many aspects of life in a busy, modern society depend on and are thoroughly bound up with publicity. People in politics, sport, business, entertainment and the media themselves need publicity, and flourish on it. And this is not just publicity for issues and causes with which people are associated or which they are pushing; it is publicity for people, individuals, personalities.[2] A clear and non-trivial example of this is the fact that nowadays the personal image of the leader of a political party is as important an electoral issue as that party's policies. These days top politicians, like top footballers and top film stars, have to be personalities. And where would the personalities be without the cult of personality generated by the media?

Yet personalities can turn against the media that feed them and complain that the press has gone too far. In many cases these complaints are justified. But often in such cases the offence is not invasion of privacy but something much more basically disturbing, like simple lies or straightforward distortions of the truth. Such behaviour by the press is contemptible, but it does not follow that there are no legitimate targets for probing by the media. Far from it. The press should critically scrutinise those who exercise power, for well beyond entertainment and providing free publicity for personalities as the actual role of the press is the central democratic function of casting a sceptical eye on the processes and personnel of politics and power and, most importantly, keeping the public informed of the results. Ordinary members of the public do not have access to this information, which is why a free and fearless press is essential to a democratic society. Unfortunately there are few examples in the world today of the press matching up to this ideal image, part of which is to scrutinise the exercise of power and also, of course, at the same time to respect privacy – where it is due.

THE NATURE OF PRIVACY

But what is privacy? One influential theory is that put forward by Sissela Bok in the context of an investigation of secrecy. Bok claims that privacy and secrecy are closely linked, yet are essentially different. Secrecy can involve a range of related concepts, including sacredness, intimacy, privacy, silence, prohibition, furtiveness and deception. The core of secrecy is, however, intentional concealment.[3]

That which is private is not always secret: the ordinary events and experiences of everyday life are not intentionally concealed but are simply maintained within the personal domain, not offered to the gaze and scrutiny of the public. Secrecy can be a means to or a form of privacy, if privacy is 'the condition of being protected from unwanted access by others'.[4] Secrecy, however, although its use by an individual could be widespread, requires a specific object – that which is concealed. Privacy is more general: it is more like a way of life, a condition (as Bok suggests), and, on this way of looking at it, a necessary (but not a sufficient) condition, for the suggestion is that it is a psychological requirement for a satisfactory life. Privacy meets a need: it offers the self protection against vulnerabilities by providing comfort and control and by strengthening the sense of identity.

According to this theory, then, privacy does not imply that there is something to hide, and certainly not that it hides a shameful secret. Privacy simply recognises the importance of not handing over the power to control one's own life to someone else. It thus relates itself to such concepts as self-fulfilment and self-respect, personal dignity and security, autonomy and identity, and in general the integrity and immunity of the person, and it differentiates itself from the consequences of its negation: feelings of defencelessness and nakedness, fear and embarrassment, bewilderment, distress and emotional upset.[5]

But although I do not wish to deny that there is much truthful insight in the psychological-need theory of privacy and in the claim that privacy is to do with the protection of the self,[6] I do believe that it is wrong to link privacy too closely with an individualistic notion of the self. For privacy as the individual's protection against others can veer off in an obsessive direction to the point where the self becomes isolated. Sandra Marshall draws our attention to the fact that in recognising the importance of privacy we are not accepting the self of the solipsist:

> the self in the sense relevant here is a social creation . . . Our sense of self is given only through our community with others . . . The thoughts and feelings which are mine must be recognised as mine by others if *I* am to have any sense of them as mine, and thus any sense of my self.[7]

But for this theory to work, what must be recognised as mine by others must be so recognised without these others knowing what it is, or even, to some extent, whether it exists. That is to say, other people have to accept that I can have (for example) beliefs that are mine, without their knowing what my beliefs on a particular subject are or even whether I have any on this topic. For clearly, if people could recognise my beliefs as mine only if they knew that I had them and what their content was, then the whole project of privacy that Marshall is supporting would collapse.

Furthermore, isn't this theory still too individualistic, in spite of the mention of 'community with others', for it seems to be a community not of association but of antagonism between self and others: the self depends on separation and distance. Recognition of the self by others is a negative conception of sociability which does not do justice to the active involvement of the self with others. Each human life is indeed the life of an individual, yet such a life is essentially public and social. We are as individuals positively and purposely bound up with other people in all areas of life.

The result is that life is a synchronic balance between the outwardness of living in society and that inner retreat we call privacy. Ideally there should certainly be a non-antagonistic equilibrium between the two, though perhaps this is one of those elusive goals the search for which makes human life such an interesting tragedy. The point of equilibrium is clearly different for different people. Lack of balance in both directions, to produce either the exhibitionist or the recluse, can be pathological, but between the two extremes is a lengthy continuum of more or less satisfactory resting points.

Another reason for rejecting an over-individualistic idea of the self in the context of privacy is that privacy itself need not be individualistic: it is not always attached to the life-condition of a lone individual. Like a secret, privacy can be shared between individuals, and in some of its manifestations must be shared, as in the case of the privacy of lovers, or just two people having a conversation.[8] In fact, a great part of life is private only in this shared sense.

Nevertheless, although privacy can be shared, it remains personal in the sense that it is a condition only of the lives of persons, that is, individual social beings. Institutions and corporations can make claims on confidentiality and secrecy, but not privacy. Of course, as Bok points out, the affairs of corporations are automatically private in so far as they are not made public, but this does not bring them within the domain or language of privacy.[9] This allows one important conclusion to be drawn at this stage. It is not legitimate for corporations to try to divert investigation of their affairs with accusations of invasion of privacy. This is an abuse of the notion of privacy.[10]

There are three (again overlapping) areas of personal life where the protection of privacy might be sought, and hence three types of privacy. The first two could be called *direct*, and the third *indirect*.

1 *Bodily or physical privacy*: this provides a space in which the body can exist, function and move, free from physical intrusions like the too close proximity of other people or bodily contact and touching, and free from observational intrusions of eyes and cameras (and other senses and sensors).
2 *Mental or communicational privacy*: this allows a person to be alone with their thoughts and feelings, wishes and desires, to keep written or electronic records of them and to communicate them to selected other people, free from eavesdropping, intrusion and other forms of psychological invasion.
3 *Informational privacy*: this provides protection for personal information which is legitimately held in the files of public and private organisations, and prevents the disclosure of such information to third parties. 'Legitimately' means not only in accordance with the law but also with the subject's knowledge and consent. Such information includes details of bank accounts, tax returns, credit status, social-security records, education records, employment records and medical records.

The distinctions I have drawn so far are not of course so clear-cut in real life. For example, someone with access to the relevant computers could obtain information about the geographical movements and spending patterns of a person who used a lot of plastic money (credit cards, switch cards, cash cards). Through this breach of informational privacy, both bodily and mental privacy would also have been invaded, though *indirectly.*

Privacy differs from secrecy in its moral status. Bok has pointed out that whereas lying is (prima facie) bad, secrecy in general is neither good nor bad but morally neutral: it is only particular cases or practices of secrecy that can be morally evaluated. But if secrecy is morally in the middle and lying is on one side of it, privacy is surely on the other side: not just prima facie good but good without qualification or exception. This follows from the fact that I have defined privacy in such a way that invasions of it are never justified.

There are well-known dangers of building a moral evaluation into a definition: it begs too many questions. But in this case the procedure seems acceptable (as well as unavoidable). It does not follow, of course, that every *claim* to the protection of privacy can be established, but it does follow that where a claim is not upheld, the behaviour or other aspect of life under consideration was never within the domain of privacy at all.

What follows from the brief examination of the nature of privacy in this section is that privacy is not a simple concept, and that its realisation is by no means simple either. It is a good, yet one whose domain has boundaries that are neither clear nor fixed. Conceptually, privacy comes up against the social nature of human life. But beyond this it comes up against the publicity-based nature of modern society, and against the requirements of a supposedly democratic political system. It is at these social and political frontiers that the role of the media becomes significant.

PRIVACY AND THE MEDIA

In considering where the media should draw the ethical boundaries of privacy, I shall look at three groups. First are personalities, those who are created and sustained by publicity. Second are people who find themselves thrust into the public eye involuntarily. Third, and most important, are politicians and similar figures who occupy positions of power in society. The distinctions are neither exhaustive nor exclusive, but a consideration of these three groups will enable most of the ground to be covered.

Once personalities were in what was called 'show business', but show business has now expanded beyond entertainment to incorporate elements of the arts, sport, politics, royalty and the media themselves. Here we find people created by publicity, who would not be who or what they are without this exposure. They range from people who are only famous for being famous to those who have genuine talents to offer to the world. All such people live on the press and off the press; they require publicity and would shrivel without it. Such people, who tend to live according to the maxim that all publicity is good publicity, cannot consistently claim the protection of privacy when they discover the negative side of the Faustian contract. When the publicity suddenly becomes painful, as it might when it concerns death, disease, a drugs bust or a brush with the income-tax authorities, claims to a right to a private life shade quickly into hypocrisy. And this, as I shall argue shortly, is outside the protection of privacy. Nevertheless, although the press does not offend against privacy in reporting such matters, it does not follow that it ought to report them. Lapses of taste are no more justifiable than invasions of privacy. Furthermore, resources are limited, and the press has more important tasks than to concern itself with senseless trivialities – among which, incidentally, I should include most of the activities of royalty.

In contrast to personalities, many people find themselves in the glare of publicity not because they have chosen it but because they are thrust into the public eye unexpectedly or even against their will. One sub-group of such people is formed by those whose interesting eminence or achievement is relatively long term or permanent: writers, artists, people at the calmer end of sport or entertainment, though perhaps the scientist who makes a breakthrough or wins a Nobel prize could stand as an example. Such people could be considered somewhat more public than the genuine 'ordinary citizens' who form the second sub-group: the disaster survivors, the relatives of someone involved in a tragic situation, the parents of a child who is a transplant patient, or, on a happier note, the pools winner. To the extent that the events that members of both sub-groups are involved in are public matters, there is no reason why the press should not seek to report them. Indeed, the circulation of general-interest information is a reasonable and legitimate activity of the media.

The United States, with its constitutional guarantee of the freedom of the press, goes further than this. 'People who are catapulted into the public eye by events are generally classified with elected officials under the privacy laws' – that is, they have no right to privacy – and furthermore, 'the courts have ruled material newsworthy because a newspaper or station carries the story'.[11] But such a principle makes the press the sole judge of what is private, and goes beyond a reasonable ethical practice for the media. When people are involved in public events there can be no objection on privacy grounds to the press reporting what is already known, together with non-intrusive background or follow-up stories. But to the extent that the people involved are not public people, they can justifiably choose to reject press advances and requests for further interviews or information and claim the protection of privacy.

I turn now to public figures like politicians and others who exercise power in society, and about them there is a good deal more to say, starting with the central question. To what extent do public people have a right to a private life? Is it true, as has been claimed in the House of Commons, that 'when one decides to become a public figure one gives up in some way a little of one's right to privacy'?[12]

This suggestion could be criticised from both sides. (a) No, one does not give up even a little of one's right to privacy. (b) No, one gives up more than a little; one gives up a lot, or even the lot.

Sissela Bok has supported the first side, even though on another occasion she has written: 'There is no clear line surrounding private life that can demarcate regions journalists ought not to explore.'[13] But in an earlier work she had offered public figures clear and considerable protection: 'Information about their marriages, their children, their opinions about others – information about their personal plans and about their motives for personal decisions – all are theirs to keep private if they wish to do so.'[14] There is some justification in this. After all, if privacy is necessary for the protection of the self and the flourishing of the individual, should not even politicians have a right to privacy? And more than this, would it not be to the benefit of society for its politicians to have selves that were flourishing rather than stressed by lack of privacy?

All this is true enough, and indicates that the genuinely personal aspects of the life of a politician should indeed be granted the protection of privacy. So in this respect the politician is no different from anyone else. But the peculiar ethical demands of political life mean that this protected area is smaller for politicians, and, furthermore, not very secure. Paradoxically, the privacy of a politician is always liable to be under scrutiny. For Bok's suggestion that what is to be regarded as private depends on the politician's own wishes is not acceptable. It would make politicians judges and juries in their own cases, whereas empirical studies of corruption show that politicians are very poor at drawing an ethically acceptable line between public life and what is properly private.[15]

An imaginary but typical case would go like this: the local politician who has received entertainment or gifts from a businessman will say (and let us allow that it is sincerely believed), 'All I was doing was accepting the generosity of a personal friend', whereas the law will say, 'No, you were taking bribes from someone in whose direction you could push contracts.' Furthermore, to demonstrate just how confused they are on the public/private distinction, corrupt officials have been known to involve their spouses and children in their activities.

At least there are statutory limits to what is permissible in local government in Britain. One of the extraordinarily unsatisfactory features of British political life is that the members of parliament who legislate for severe anti-corruption controls on local politics and politicians would not dream of imposing such standards on themselves. Indeed, with very few constraints they are free to sell their services to the highest bidder.[16] Thus the world of parliamentary politics easily leads into what some would consider the real location of power, the financial world. Here there has been a plethora of recent scandals for the press to investigate, and it must not allow itself to be distracted by ritual incantations of the public/private distinction. For again this distinction is difficult to draw, as is shown by the case of Robert Maxwell, whose public and 'family' businesses were enmeshed in a single web of disaster.

It follows that Bok's account of what is personal and private will not do, and the conclusion seems to be that politicians and other public figures of power cannot expect much privacy. But is this going too far? For many commentators on this subject have suggested that there is a reasonable middle way, along the lines of the criterion put forward in the following:

> In 1976 . . . the Press Council published its declaration on individual privacy, which stated that the publication of information about someone's private life, without that person's consent, was only acceptable where there is a 'legitimate public interest overriding the right to privacy'. Even a public figure was entitled to respect for his or her privacy, except where circumstances relating to his [*sic*] private life could affect the performance of his [*sic*] duties or public confidence in him or his [*sic*] position.[17]

In other words, it is a matter of relevance. Only where performance in private life is relevant to performance in public life is private life a proper object of concern or investigation. Where it is irrelevant, there is the outer limit of privacy.

But does such a criterion offer any genuine assistance? Leaving aside the obvious difficulty that the relevance of a person's private life cannot be known unless it is investigated, there is the question of the psychological and moral dualism implied in the public/private distinction. Is the public person a different person from the private person?

Politicians and other public persons should have their personal lives protected only on the assumption that the way they behave in their public lives – the character, principles, attitudes, beliefs and virtues they display – are not only quite distinct from but are also greatly superior to their behaviour and character in their private lives. No one could claim that this assumption is true a priori. And if it is taken as making an empirical claim, it must be tested empirically, case by case. Either way, the assumption is implausible. I acknowledge, indeed I insist upon, the fact that the unity of the person sought by philosophers and psychologists as the sibling of personal identity is a chimera. Nevertheless, a person does not neatly divide into two characters, the public and the private. And (to return to the difficulty just raised) if a person did divide in this way, this could be found out only by investigating both sides of the division.

But is this too high a standard, especially if applied to that area of perennial interest, sex? Would not such a standard have destroyed the career of John F. Kennedy, not to mention David Lloyd George or even Harold Macmillan (because of his wife's activities) and a host of others whose still-living status means they definitely may not be mentioned? The standard is high, but it is not unreasonable to impose it on those who seek positions of such power, as several contenders for the presidency of the United States have discovered to their chagrin during the last decade or so.

But in such cases the target of the press has often been not so much the sexual (mis)conduct itself as the surrounding hypocrisy and double standards. Even if politicians and similar public figures can claim some privacy for their personal lives, the protection should not be available when they indulge in double standards. Present and recent senior members of the British government regularly intone support for 'the family' and family values, condemn 'permissiveness' and attack one-parent families for their corrupting and delinquent consequences. Such stances are (among other things equally bad) sheer hypocrisy. For many of these moralists are into their second marriage or that of their spouse, a position that is frequently not possible without leaving one-parent families behind. Contrary to their professed utterances politicians accept the inevitability and desirability of separation and divorce in many cases, and are also happy to accept the benefits in their own cases. There is no reason why the press should feel inhibited in exposing such double standards.

But the real problem with sexual peccadilloes is neither their intrinsic nature nor their consequences but the prurient and sanctimonious atmosphere in which they subsist. Thus while it is right that allegations of sexual misconduct against Clarence Thomas should have been fully investigated before he was confirmed as a justice of the United States Supreme Court, it does not follow that every detail of the investigation should be broadcast coast-to-coast. It would not be right for the media to cover up real or alleged sexual scandals, nor to blow them up out of all proportion. What is needed within society as a whole is a more moderate and healthy attitude towards human sexuality and sexual relations, both heterosexual and homosexual, and if this came about, the need for hypocrisy and double standards perceived by many in public life would diminish and eventually disappear. One clear ethical responsibility on the media – one they are a long way from fully accepting – is to fight bigotry and hypocrisy and to promote a new enlightened atmosphere about sex.

PRIVACY AND CONSENT

Consent is highly relevant to the issue of privacy. On the one hand it has been called 'a vital element';[18] on the other it has been pointed out that 'it would be wrong to conclude that journalists ought to write only about persons who have given their consent'.[19]

Some distinctions are needed. In the case of personalities, those who live by publicity, consent can be assumed. In the case of public people, for whom I have already argued the protection of privacy is at best very limited, consent can again be assumed outside any small protected domain. In cases involving criminality, corruption, hypocrisy and unethical behaviour, consent is not needed. In all other cases, those concerning ordinary people who find themselves thrust into the public eye, or family members who are innocent of any relevant involvement, consent should be a requirement.

And media ethics should borrow from medical ethics and insist on the consent being informed. One consequence of this is that it immediately rules out any form of deception by journalists in cases in which consent is required or can be assumed. In such cases deception would amount to dishonesty. In cases in which consent is not required, cases involving the corrupt or the hypocritical, the issue is less clear. Some form of deception might be required if any investigation was to take place at all. Perhaps the answer is that deception is acceptable so long as it does not become dishonesty. But the ethical line is difficult to draw.

PRIVACY, ETHICS AND POLITICS

The press has a difficult course to steer between privacy and publicity. But any suggestion that it should be forced into line by a statutory right to privacy would have, I believe, disastrous consequences. The British press is already too restricted by the repressive use of laws of official secrets, confidence, libel and contempt of court, and to add privacy to this list would be to invite further misuse of the law by public figures with something to hide. For example, Robert Maxwell prevented any serious investigation of his affairs by the constant and immediate presentation of libel writs, and, bearing in mind that much of his business was carried on through so-called 'private' companies, no doubt would have added an avalanche of privacy writs if they had been available.

No, it is ethics, not law, that should protect privacy, but a reasonable code of ethics would also not inhibit investigative journalism, but encourage it. In other words, rather than containing a negative list of restrictions, the code should have a positive emphasis on the role of the press within a democratic society.

Information is the substance and sustenance of a democratic society. 'Information' should be understood in a wide sense: not just factual information but also the opinion, comment, criticism, speculation, discussion and debate that are needed to keep democracy healthy and society free and fair. A democratic society therefore requires freedom of information and freedom of expression, and this gives the press its vital role, that of providing people with the information that they need to know in order to be democratic citizens. It does not follow that people should be forced to be politically active, nor that the press has only a political role. There is more to life than politics, and the press can be entertaining and relaxing as well as informative.

A democratic society is an ideal. In reality there is always slippage from the ideal. Here again the emphasis should be on the positive role of the press in promoting a fairer society, by attacking discrimination, hypocrisy and bigotry, for example, or by combating political corruption and corporate fraud. It is the big-time enemies of a fair and democratic society that should be the targets of the press, not trivial details about the lives of personalities. Unaccountable power is the enemy of democracy, and the investigation of both the use and abuse of power can never be an invasion of privacy.

Of course in a democratic society there will be protection for the privacy of citizens. But in a genuinely democratic society it would be unthinkable for the press to invade anyone's privacy. It would have better things to do, and would be content to do them.[20]

NOTES

1 Privacy and the press is what I shall concentrate on, meaning the newspaper and periodical press. Much of what I say is also applicable to the journalistic activities of the electronic media, but there are differences, as in the UK at least, radio and television are much more tightly controlled by statutory regulations and supervisory bodies.
2 In this chapter I use 'personality' always to mean 'person in the public eye', 'celebrity', etc., and not 'distinctive personal character'.
3 Sissela Bok, *Secrets: On the Ethics of Concealment and Revelation* (Oxford and New York, Oxford University Press, 1984), pp. 5–6.
4 ibid., p. 10.
5 For an account of privacy that links it with the self, identity and autonomy, see Sandra E. Marshall, 'Public Bodies, Private Selves', *Journal of Applied Philosophy*, 5 (1988), pp. 147–58.
6 ibid., p. 153.
7 ibid., p. 152.
8 But for a criticism of the idea that intimate relationships are *created* by sharing what is private, see Marshall, op. cit., pp. 151–2.
9 Bok, op. cit., p. 13.
10 This abuse was institutionalised in the terms of reference of the Younger Committee on Privacy which reported to parliament in 1972: 'To consider whether legislation is needed to give further protection to the individual citizen and to commercial and industrial interests against intrusions into privacy by private persons and organisations, or by companies, and to make recommendations.' There was also a further abuse here, in that the language was designed to ensure that the more serious threats to privacy from government organisations, the security services or the police would be excluded from the terms of reference.
11 Clifford G. Christians, Kim B. Rotzoll and Mark Fackler, *Media Ethics: Cases and Moral Reasoning*, 3rd edn (New York, Longman, 1991), p. 138.
12 Conservative MP R.C. Mitchell in the debate on the Younger Committee Report, House of Commons, 13 July 1972; reproduced in Mervyn Jones (ed.), *Privacy* (Newton Abbot, David & Charles, 1974), p. 193.
13 Bok, op. cit., p. 252.
14 Sissela Bok, *Lying: Moral Choice in Public and Private Life* (London, Quartet, 1980), p. 176.
15 See Alan Doig, *Corruption and Misconduct in Contemporary British Politics* (London, Penguin, 1984).
16 Mark Hollingsworth, *MPs for Hire: The Secret World of Political Lobbying* (London, Bloomsbury, 1991).
17 Patricia Hewitt, *Privacy: The Information Gatherers* (London, National Council for Civil Liberties, 1977), p. 84.
18 Mervyn Jones, 'Introduction', in Jones, op. cit., p. 14.

19 Bok, *Secrets*, p. 252.
20 This chapter is a revised version of a paper first presented at the 1990 Conference of the Society for Applied Philosophy. I would like to thank the participants for discussion, especially Robin Attfield, Ruth Chadwick and Shyli Karin-Frank.

Chapter 7

Honesty in investigative journalism

Jennifer Jackson

> The public's right to know of events of public importance and interest is the overriding mission of the mass media.
>
> (Society of Professional Journalists, *Code of Ethics*, 1973)

> The press is the most important counterbalance we possess against the secretiveness of government and commercial institutions.
>
> (Sissela Bok, *Secrets*)

Reporting the truth is said to be 'at the heart of the journalistic enterprise'.[1] What, then, if the truth can only be found out by deceptive stratagems? Is not lying an indispensable stratagem for investigative journalism? Only by posing, by pretending to be what they are not and to know what they do not, do journalists succeed in penetrating secretive powerful organisations and in securing the evidence they need to expose corruption and mischief.

Some doctors claim exemption from a strict rule against lying in as much as they on occasion have to lie (so they say) to fulfil their overriding duty to patients to do them no harm. Might not journalists claim to be similarly exempted: that they sometimes 'have to' lie to fulfil their overriding duty to the public to unearth and reveal important truths?

The topic of honesty in investigative journalism covers questions about what honesty requires or permits journalists to do, first to get their stories and second in communicating their stories (for example, whether, in the second case, it is dishonest deliberately to suppress a suspect's racial identity so as not to incite racial hatred, though doubtless the public would be keenly interested to know). Here, I propose to discuss honesty only in the former news-gathering context.

In order to clarify what honesty requires of people in general, of journalists in particular, it would be helpful to establish why honesty matters; why it is held to be a moral virtue; and what its status as a moral virtue signifies. Discussion of these questions should enable us to specify more precisely what is wrong with lying and hence to establish whether lying is always wrong. Let us proceed then to consider the importance of honesty and, in the light of our findings, to consider the wrongness of lying; and then to enquire into the alleged rightness of investigative journalists lying in the cause of truth.

THE IMPORTANCE OF HONESTY

Social co-operation depends on our willingness to act within certain constraints in our various individual and joint pursuits: what we may call 'the constraints of justice'. These most obviously include constraints on the use of force and fraud. Fraud destroys trust. We are able to trust one another only in so far as the duty to be truthful, i.e., not to lie, is generally acknowledged.

But it is one thing to see the need for such a constraint, quite another to resolve effectively to live within its limitations. There are many temptations to deviate from the duty to be truthful and not only for those among us who are worldly and self-seeking. If this duty is to be acknowledged in practice, it needs to be anchored in people's characters. Hence the need to cultivate honesty as a virtue, as a disposition which binds us emotionally, not just intellectually, to truthfulness.

We need to cultivate in others the disposition to be honest – but in ourselves? As Plato's Thrasymachus observes, 'justice is another man's good', i.e., we benefit directly from the just dispositions of others but only indirectly, if at all, from our own. Maybe, as moralists (naturally) insist, the policy of counterfeiting a concern for justice while free-riding at others' expense is too risky to be rational. Be that as it may, at least we can see that we need to cultivate in others on whom we need to rely an attachment to truthfulness that is genuine. Honesty, then, is a moral virtue and one which we all have an interest in promoting: its function is to preserve trust, and trust is a social necessity.

But not every practice that can cause deception or may be engaged in to cause deception need be regarded as subversive of trust, for example 'the willing suspension of belief' in poetry, art and theatre; adorning ourselves with mock jewellery or our homes with plastic flowers; the distressing of reproduction furniture to give it an antique appearance; cosmetic surgery, etc. Of course, none of these need even cause deception let alone be intended to do so. There need be nothing secretive or deceptive about your arranging to have an unsightly wart surgically removed from your face.

But even where there is an intent to deceive, there may not be any abuse of trust. Contrast allowing your customers to assume that a piece of furniture is older than it is because of its distress marks and allowing visitors to your house to make the same false assumption. The issue of trust may arise in the one context but not the other. Perhaps it is none of your visitors' business to know and they do not rely on you to correct them: whereas, arguably, it is your buyers' business to know and you, as a seller, have an obligation not only not to lie, but not to intentionally mislead either.

Only if trust is being placed in you does the possibility of your taking advantage of it even arise. Are there not occasions on which you might deliberately deceive others who could not plausibly be said to be putting trust in you, nor to have any right to rely on you but who might still deliberately be led by you into making false suppositions?

Suppose, for example, that you are a British tourist holidaying in an Arab land when some international crisis erupts. Not wishing to be conspicuously British (lest you be attacked or taken hostage) you might decide to converse only in French when in public. Or suppose that you are a reporter wanting to observe what is going on without anyone noticing that you are a reporter (lest you be attacked or, at any rate, escorted off the premises). So as not to make yourself conspicuous you might dress up (in white coat or black suit) or dress down (in jeans and T-shirt) as appropriate.[2] In both kinds of situations you would hope for, and intend, people to make false assumptions. But could these people be said to have been relying on you to speak your own language or to dress in a manner that revealed your vocation? Surely not.

If, though, upon being challenged you were to lie to them about your identity or to produce forged papers, that, surely, would be quite a different matter. Your explicit assurances would *invite* them to believe what was false. You would appear, thus, to be giving them a right to trust in you, a trust you would proceed intentionally to take advantage of. Of course, the line between the explicit spoken lie and an intentional deception which involves neither telling nor acting a lie may not always be easy to draw. Compare infiltrating a military barracks by posing in a borrowed uniform you are not entitled to wear, and infiltrating a medical conference at which you know journalists would not be welcome by introducing yourself (truthfully) as Dr ____, thereby allowing people to assume (incorrectly) that you are medically qualified when in fact your doctorate is in media studies.

In what follows we will restrict our discussion of deception in investigative journalism to practices which involve outright lying; the practice of undercover reporting being a characteristic form in which this occurs, as where a journalist poses, for example, as a patient so as to check out rumours of patient neglect, or as an illegal migrant worker to spy on factory working conditions.

Lies are a most explicit form of intentional deception where the aim must always be to take advantage of another's trust. Is it possible, even so, to justify the telling of some lies?

Let us distinguish justifications from excuses as follows: a justification for what one has done purports to demonstrate that what one did was not, in the circumstances, wrong. An excuse for what one has done purports to demonstrate that one is not (so much) to blame for what one has done even if what one did was wrong. Excuses take the form of demonstrating either that one did not act (altogether) voluntarily or that one did not act (altogether) knowingly. In the case of lying, of course, it being essentially intentional deception, only the former type of excuse is possible.

Here we are concerned with the possibility of justifying, rather than excusing, the telling of lies: whether someone who is honest, who genuinely cares about truthfulness, may still *rightly* choose to lie in certain circumstances.

The wrongness of lying, I have derived from our common fundamental need to maintain, by not betraying, trust: a need which is the basis of the duty we are under to be truthful. But while liars inevitably take advantage of others' trust, are there not circumstances in which taking advantage is not taking *unjust* advantage, that is, is not in fact a 'betrayal' of trust?

Suppose, for instance, that those of whom we take advantage are known to us not themselves to be trustworthy: are they then *entitled* to trust us? If liars forfeit the right to trust, we, in lying to them, do *them* no injustice.

Then again, people may waive the right not to be lied to, as in games of bluff, in which case we are entitled to take advantage of their trust – we have their 'consent', so to speak. And if lying to those who allow us to do so is permissible, might we not sometimes also be justified in *assuming* the consent of those to whom we lie – where we lie from benign motives in circumstance in which any reasonable person would prefer to have been lied to?

Moreover, even if the persons to whom we lie neither have forfeited the right not to be lied to nor can be assumed to waive that right, since the right is anyway not absolute, we still may not be taking an *unjust* advantage of them. Thus their right not to be lied to may conflict with another right, for example, some other people's right to have confidences kept, which in the circumstances are overriding: circumstances may make it not just permissible but morally necessary for us to lie.

Here then are three different types of justification: for lying to liars, for lying to 'consenters' and for telling morally necessary lies. Let us examine each of these types of justification in turn and consider whether honest and responsible journalists must scorn them all.

LYING TO LIARS

If we concede that it is all right to lie to liars we might as well concede simply that it is all right to lie, for virtually everyone tells a lie sometimes (except, of course, George Washington). We might distinguish between habitual liars and occasional liars and say it is all right to lie to the former but not to the latter; but such a ruling would be impracticable to apply, it being so unclear who falls into which category. Moreover, if lying is permissible to some liars and not to others we need some explanation why.

It might be argued that it is only permissible for us to lie to those who have lied to us, the underlying rationale being that justice permits us to do as we are done by, to retaliate, to pay people back in their own coin – the justice of an eye for an eye. On this conception of justice, presumably, not only is it permitted for us to lie to those who lie to us but likewise to murder those who attempt to murder us, eat those who attempt to eat us, etc. Even if we would endorse this conception of what justice permits, though, it would not follow that in lying to those who had lied to us, we would be doing no wrong – only, that we might be doing *them* no wrong.[3]

The same deed, after all, may be unjust in more than one way: stealing from your hosts offends against both their property rights and against their hospitality rights. Stealing from people who are not your hosts is still wrong. In what way (or ways), then, may our lying to liars still be unjust even if the injustice is not to the lied-to?

Sissela Bok remarks on the proverbial difficulty of making one's first lie the last: 'It is easy, a wit observed, to tell a lie, but hard to tell only one.'[4] Certainly investigative journalists' adopting disguises in the cause of detection can hardly but embroil them in telling and acting many lies, not just to the persons being spied upon (who, we might assume, deserve no better), but also to their spouses and children.

Quite aside from one lie generating the need for further lies (the first lie 'must be thatched with another or it will rain through'[5]) there is also a difficulty over restricting the aim of our lies just to those whom we seek to deceive.[6] Other people, onlookers, although we do not lie to them, may be equally taken in by the lie we tell.

There is an important difference to be noted here, though, between those whom we have to include in our aim (as where the journalists' ploy of posing as a domestic in order to gain access to the spied-upon's home necessitates lying to the spied-upon's spouse) and those who happen accidentally though foreseeably to be deceived by the lies which are not directed at them. The former we lie to; the latter we only allow to be deceived. While we are under a duty to be truthful, to tell no lies, are we also under a duty, another duty, to prevent deception?

Since, as we have already noted, not only allowing deception but causing deception, even intentionally causing deception, is not necessarily unjust, we cannot have a duty to prevent deception as such. We may still have a duty to prevent injustice and hence to prevent deception which is unjust. But this latter duty, to prevent unjust deception, will be of a different kind from the duty to tell no lies: it will be what philosophers call an 'imperfect' duty. The duty to be truthful, to tell no lies, though, is a 'perfect' duty. It is clearly possible, not necessarily easy, to follow a rule never to tell lies, whereas a rule 'never allow deception' hardly even makes sense.

Perfect duties need not be absolute but they are precise and determinate in what they require of us. They are straightforwardly fulfillable: they can be 'done' without remainder, so to speak. Thus, you can know that you have kept all the appointments which you had made for today. Imperfect duties, on the other hand, are somewhat vague and open-ended. You may spend the day dutifully caring for your aged parent and yet not only might you have been equally dutiful in acting quite differently *vis-à-vis* your parent throughout the day, but no matter how exemplary your attentiveness has been, there will still remain other dutiful things you could do or might have done in addition.

Because of the open-ended and indeterminate character of imperfect duties we necessarily have a degree of discretion over how we act on them. Thus an honest person may see an opportunity to prevent unjust deception yet allow it to pass. Honest people may pursue policies although they foresee that in carrying them through they will undoubtedly (albeit unintentionally) generate in some innocent persons a degree of mistrust. Being honest, they will not be indifferent to this consequence but they may still regard the harm they allow as outweighed by the benefits to be achieved. Perfect duties do not admit of a similar discretion over how and when to act on them: you cannot pick and choose to whom to be truthful bearing in mind overall consequences.

As a justification, then, for journalists lying in the cause of informing the public of important matters, for example, of corruption in high places, the argument that those to whom the journalists would lie are themselves liars is doubtfully relevant and, in any case, not conclusive. It is hardly relevant unless those to whom the journalists would lie have lied specifically to them – otherwise the justification for lying to liars (by way of retaliation) does not apply. And even if the journalists are entitled to lie by way of retaliation, can they restrict their lies to the legitimate targets – the more elaborate the hoax plotted, the less feasible is such an economy in lying. Then further we must ask what other harm can be expected to result from the lies to be told and whether these harms would be sufficiently compensated for by the benefits aimed at – whether, for instance, there are not alternative ways of discovering the truth that would not generate (so much) distrust.

LYING TO CONSENTERS

Rights may be waived. You may thereby be justified in doing what would otherwise be contrary to duty. But only if the waiver is acting *reasonably* in giving consent, otherwise the genuineness of the consent becomes doubtful: is it free? Is it informed? On the other hand, someone who withholds consent unreasonably cannot all the same be deemed to be consenting – you would need some other justification for lying to such a person. Presumably, we act reasonably in waiving our right not to be lied to only if the permission we are extending relates to a quite clearly defined area of intercourse – as in games of bluff where the permission relates only to the playing of the game: you may lie to your opponents about the cards in your hand but not about the content of the drinks you put in their hands.

Clearly, since a lie is ineffective if it is recognised when told, there has to be some distance between the time at which permission is sought and that at which the permitted lie is told: consent must be either in advance or retrospective.

ADVANCE CONSENT

There are circumstances, games aside, where we may rationally permit others to intentionally deceive us, even if need be to lie to us. There may be an informed public consensus in favour of unmarked police cars, plain-clothes detectives, clandestine health and safety inspections and the regular use of placebos in the testing of new drugs on patients – not that any of these practices would *normally* necessitate telling lies.

The use of placebos, indeed, need not even involve any deception. Patients may be invited to enter a trial on the understanding that some of them will be given placebos only. At the very point of administering the drugs, medical attendants could remind their patients that what they were imbibing might or might not be a placebo.

Some trials, though, might necessitate a more elaborate pretence and some might only be feasible if consent were sought retrospectively. At any rate, advance consent, provided it is given freely and informedly, would seem to render subsequent deception, even lying, if that were necessary to deceive effectively, permissible and morally unproblematic.

RETROSPECTIVE CONSENT

Sometimes, when it has not been feasible to seek consent in advance it is sought 'retrospectively', so to speak. The media might comply with a request from the police to release false information so as to lure kidnappers into a trap. Subsequently the public might be 'debriefed' and its approval sought and gained retrospectively for the media's complicity.

Suppose doctors seek to establish the extent of non-compliance by patients following through their prescriptions. Doctors might have merely anecdotal evidence to suggest that many patients do not comply and do not own up to their own non-compliance, a source of worry to their doctors who can only guess whether their patients' symptoms persist in spite of the medicines or not, and a source of worry to the public at large in so far as medicines prescribed and not used are a wasted expense for the health service.

An experiment might, then, be devised to test compliance which would necessarily be clandestine – pursued without advance consent. A harmless tracer substance might be put in the medication which would enable doctors to measure accurately over a period their patients' compliance. Here consent, if sought at all, would have to be sought retrospectively.

What constitutes retrospective consent? People may be deemed to have consented in retrospect only if upon being 'debriefed' they approve of what was done and are no way resentful. We are justified in relying on obtaining retrospective consent only where obtaining it in advance is not feasible. Whereas advance consent enables liars to know when they lie that their lie is not wrong, where consent is to be sought retrospectively liars take a risk: though they intend to debrief and seek retrospective consent, they cannot be sure that it will be forthcoming and hence whether their lies will turn out to have been justified.

How necessary is reliance on retrospective consent in journalism? Journalists may find that many people are greatly inhibited by the knowledge that their words are being recorded on tape – even if they are assured in advance that they can edit the tape and that nothing from them will be used without their agreement. Interviewees typically might prove to be much more spontaneous, interesting and informative if they learn only after the event that they have been taped. Then too, for some undercover work you cannot safely seek consent except retrospectively lest those whom you take into your confidence accidentally betray you.[7]

As we have noted, while you cannot assume that you have consent except in circumstances where it would be reasonable to give it, neither can you assume that you have consent merely on the grounds that giving it would be reasonable. Hence there is still a risk in relying on retrospective consent even if it is obvious (to you) that in the circumstances it would be reasonable for the deceived to give it. Hence, furthermore, if you happen to know (or ought to know) that the person whom you propose to deceive is (relevantly) unreasonable you are *not* justified in assuming that you have consent.

Suppose, for example, that a wife hides her husband's cigarettes from him: he has earnestly assured her (and his doctor) of his determination to stop smoking. In a moment of weakness he is seeking them and appeals to his wife: does she know where they are? Has she hidden them? If she lies, and later (presumably much later when he has finally succeeded in overcoming the habit) confesses, he might, perhaps unreasonably, resent the deceit she has practised on him. It would not follow that her lie was unjustified: maybe her duty to protect his health overrode her duty to be truthful. But at least she could not now justify her lie on the grounds that were he reasonable he would consent retrospectively – and if his resentment was entirely predictable, then whatever justification she might have had would require another basis than consent. Such another basis might indeed be the necessity of lying to fulfil a higher duty.

MORALLY NECESSARY LIES

Perfect duties, I have argued, admit of no discretion: their requirements are specific and the necessity of doing them constrains how we may pursue our various aims, including our virtuous aims. If you are a doctor, you have an (imperfect) duty to care for your children. But how you proceed in acting on these duties day-to-day is circumscribed by the various perfect duties that you are also bound by, for example, the promises that you have made.

If you have promised to do three things today, then three things you 'must' do and your obligation to do the third is no way lessened or cancelled out by your having done two of them (any more than your obligation not to lie to patient *C* is any any way lessened or cancelled out by your having not lied to patient *A* nor to patient *B*). You are, on the other hand, entitled to pick and choose to some extent how you distribute your caring activities among your patients and the fact that you have spent the night by the bedside of one patient may well lessen or cancel out your obligation to hurry on to the next patient.

In adopting this notion of perfect duties which limit what are morally permissible means to even worthy ends, we need not, indeed cannot, insist that these perfect duties are 'absolute', that is, exceptionless. One perfect duty may after all on occasion conflict with another in which case one of them must give: they cannot both oblige if, in the circumstances, fulfilling both is impossible. Even perfect duties of the same type may conflict: your promise to *A* and your promise to *B* as in Philippa Foot's example, where having committed yourself to be best man at two weddings you find that these are unexpectedly fixed for the same day and you cannot attend both.[8]

Breaking a promise to one promisee in such circumstances is morally justified: it is morally necessary. Disappointed promisees have no right to complain: their trust has not been betrayed – unless, of course, you were in some way negligent in committing yourself and not anticipating or in some way forestalling the coincidence.

Can imperfect duties also override perfect ones? Might we not be justified in breaking a promise or telling a lie to avert some disaster or to achieve a singular benefit? In such circumstances we might, of course, be able to get (advance or retrospective) consent and justify our failure to fulfil our duty that way. But suppose that it is obvious to us that consent is not or would not be given – the party who has a claim on us is unreasonable.

We might still regard the imperfect duty to be more compelling. But even if we defend giving it preference, we cannot claim that in the circumstances we 'have to' give it priority – not at least if we stand by the view that imperfect duties to prevent harm and produce benefit allow us some discretion over how we fulfil them. Thus though I find myself in a situation where I see that I could by lying avert a disaster, I am not morally obliged to tell the lie – even if I see no other way. All the same, the lie may be permissible (not 'wrong'). Let us label lies that might be justified in this way 'judicious' lies: lies which are (rightly) judged to be permissible on the grounds that in the circumstances the end justifies the means.

JUDICIOUS LIES

The idea that ends can never justify the non-fulfilment of a perfect duty offends against common sense. Are not some lies less serious than others? Some promises, less weighty? Surely only fanatics about promise-keeping hold that every promise binds, come what may.

On the other hand, the idea that morality permits us to pick and choose what promises we keep or on what occasions we are truthful, smacks of expedience – recall Bertrand Russell's jibe against Aristotle's doctrine of the mean: 'There was once a mayor who had adopted Aristotle's doctrine; at the end of his term of office he made a speech saying that he had endeavoured to steer the narrow line between partiality on the one hand and impartiality on the other.'[9]

How firm, then, should the constraints of justice which are perfect duties be? Only as firm, presumably, as they have to be, but how firm is that? Our answer here will naturally reflect our understanding of human nature and of what G.J. Warnock broadly calls 'the human predicament'.[10]

I have suggested that the mere intellectual appreciation of the necessity we share in maintaining trust is not enough to wed us to the requisite restraints. We need to develop an allegiance to truthfulness which is in part emotional: we need to hate lies. Only then will we stand firm when the end does *not* justify the means.

Yet our allegiance to truthfulness needs also to be in part rational; it needs to be reflective, judicious. Thus while it will not *normally* even occur to people of honest disposition that the end they seek might justify telling a lie, such people can recognise that in quite exceptional circumstances, the end they have in view does justify their lying. They will of course reach such a decision reluctantly and with caution (bearing in mind the difficulties of judging situations fairly and without bias).

PROMISE-KEEPING, TRUTHFULNESS AND TRUST

Hitherto I have juxtaposed the duty to be truthful and the duty to keep promises as examples of perfect duties. But while both are perfect duties there may be important differences between them, in how they relate to trust, and consequently in how strictly we should consider ourselves to be obligated by them – how readily we should allow imperfect duties to override them. There are a number of reasons why we should expect judicious lying to be much more of a rarity than judicious promise-breaking.

Charles Fried observes: 'Every lie is a broken promise, and the only reason this seems strained is that in lying the promise is made and broken at the same moment.'[11] But not every broken promise is a lie. Lying is essentially intentional:

> One can only lie intentionally – it is not possible to lie inadvertently or as a known but unwanted side effect of some other purpose. To be sure, it is possible to create erroneous impressions as a side effect or inadvertently, but then one is not lying.[12]

Thus one's will is more closely bound in the telling of a lie than it need be in the breaking of a promise. Inadvertent injustice may be no less blameworthy than intentional injustice. Yet someone who is *prepared* to act unjustly is more of a threat to trust.

Moreover since we realise that people may easily break their promises without meaning to, we do not rely on many promises that much nor consequently feel all that let down if they are not fulfilled. Of course, some promises are quite specific, solemnly undertaken and hugely important to the parties involved. But there are a host of promises and half-promises which are vague and imprecise both in what they bind us to and about the conditions under which we remain bound.

Then too, as we are more vulnerable to hidden dangers than visible ones, we have more to fear from lying than from promise-breaking. Nothing is more damaging to trust than suspicion. Lying breeds suspicion because it involves concealment. Promise-breaking, though, need not be in the least furtive: even where we act unjustly in failing to keep a promise we may not be acting in any way dishonestly.

There is a general difficulty about establishing a person's trustworthiness since, as Diego Gambetta says, trust is 'predicated not on evidence but on the lack of *contrary* evidence'.[13] Gambetta observes: 'while it is never that difficult to find evidence of untrustworthy behaviour, it is virtually impossible to prove its positive mirror image'.[14] Even so, in testimony to a person's trustworthiness we might be able, and it would be relevant, to add to the apparent lack of contrary evidence a recitation of promises the person has not broken, whereas the idea that one might similarly lend support to a person's truthfulness by compiling a list of the lies the person has not told is nonsensical. Thus the discovery that someone has lied to us once, has a disproportionate effect on our trust in them. We reckon that where only one lie is spied many more may be hidden. Desdemona's protestations of honesty cannot on their own convince even the impartial spectator given the undisputed evidence that she has already deceived her father for love of Othello.

If, as I have been arguing, lying is characteristically more damaging to trust than is promise-breaking, we should expect the occasions for judicious lying to be more of a rarity. They may also be more difficult for us to identify – for the following reason.

In deciding whether a specific lie would be judicious we have to weigh the importance of the good at which we aim by telling it against the harm involved in or arising from its being told. Just because we do not intend or expect to be caught out lying, we are less likely to judge reliably. In our confidence that we are not in fact going to be made publicly accountable, our judgement that what we propose to do would stand the test of publicity may be overhastily reached.[15] If the lie is not going to be discovered, telling it will do no harm to the general level of trust in our community, nor need amends be made to those individuals whose trust we betray. Only the possibility that we are harming ourselves, undermining our own trustworthiness, remains, and as Sissela Bok observes we are especially apt to underestimate the seriousness of such risks:

> Bias skews all judgement, but never more so than in the search for good reasons to deceive. Not only does it combine with ignorance and uncertainty so that liars are apt to overestimate their own good will, high motives, and chances to escape detection; it leads also to overconfidence in their own imperviousness to the personal entanglements, worries, and loss of integrity which might so easily beset them.[16]

With open promise-breaking, promise-breaking that is free of deceit, on the other hand, we realise that we are going to be called to account. That prospect may naturally 'concentrate the mind' and make our inward rehearsal of the publicity test more considered – hence, more reliable than a mere thought-experiment.[17]

A note of caution is in order here concerning the 'test of publicity' – what exactly is it and why does it matter? Is there any point, after all, in testing our views against the opinions of others, unless their views are authoritative and reliable? Is the public at large authoritative on moral matters? Does public debate on matters of morals conduce to enlightenment? May it not rather generate more heat than light?

Consultation with a select portion of the public, namely, with people of apparent goodwill who are reflective and relevantly informed, is another matter. But even with them (assuming that *they* are identifiable), achieving reliable conclusions is not a matter of counting heads, the heads of 'the wise and good'. Since even *within* such a select group there is moral controversy, we cannot entirely trust their opinions when they happen to converge.

Socrates is perhaps the most memorable and pertinacious advocate of the publicity test properly applied, and he was also properly contemptuous of its misuse, of referendums on matters of principle or of relying on the opinion of even wise and good individuals such as Gorgias. What he did appreciate was the value of exposing one another's views to open criticism, of subjecting them to scrutiny in discussion, in dialogue. The point then in consulting others on matters of principle is not that they may know better, but that through discussion we and they may get to know better, even if, like Socrates, what we jointly discover is only a greater awareness of the limitations of our own understanding.

But while I think that we should, like Socrates, scorn the idea that popular opinion is in any way authoritative on matters of principle – for example, as to the rights and wrongs of abortion or of killing animals for sport – there may be, all the same, a distinct particular value in exploring attitudes of the public at large and encouraging and attending to public debate in relation to specific moral dilemmas and how people think that they should be handled. The purpose of studying what people say here is not to test out the reasoning which underlies our own principles but to acquire relevant information. To establish whether in a specific situation lying would be judicious we need to know, for example, whether there is no alternative route that we can take which does not involve lying. We need also to know just how damaging taking advantage of people's trust is likely to be in the case in question.

There are then two distinct roles a publicity test may play: to check how our reasoning stands up to analysis in discussion and to check the reliability of the information on which we base our judgements, for example, as to the necessity of the lie or the degree to which it undermines others' trust.

Despite the value of the publicity test it would seem that when we find ourselves in a situation which might seem to warrant a judicious lie, we are confined to the mere thought-experiment mode of publicity test. Even so, there may be a difference between the predicament of benign doctors who are contemplating telling a judicious lie and public-spirited investigative journalists who do so. Whereas doctors might not normally expect ever to have to own up to the benign lies they tell their patients, journalists who engage in undercover reporting know that almost certainly they will have to own up: certainly if they publish their story they will have to explain how they came by insider information. Moreover journalists may need to debrief those upon whom they have spied, not just by way of apology (assuming that apology may be due even for lies which are judicious), but also to obtain these people's comments on, and explanations of, their own actions.[18]

Yet while the prospect of eventual publicity should ease the difficulty journalists have in judging whether the lies they consider telling to get their stories are justifiable, such judgements are still difficult. A calculation has to be made, for instance, of how far the eventual debriefing can be expected to dispel the sense of betrayal experienced by those who are to be deceived (since only if the good to be achieved outweighs the harm done in order to achieve it can the lie be judicious). But it is easy to underestimate the sense of betrayal, the resentment, the feelings of powerlessness, the general loss of trust experienced by those who discover that they have been duped, even if they were duped without personal malice and in a good cause. The anger evoked in victims of non-malign deception when they are debriefed may come as something of a shock to journalists when they do own up.[19]

There are, then, formidable difficulties about establishing if a lie one would tell is judicious. But the difficulties we have found are practical in character; they require practical remedies.

THE PUBLICITY TEST AND CASE STUDIES

The obvious difficulty, as I have noted, about finding a practical remedy, is how to ascertain if the particular lie you contemplate telling would be judicious without 'giving it away'. Consultations that do not go beyond your own conscience or the consciences of your peers are no substitute for more public soundings and comment.[20] But lying has to be private.

Nevertheless, you might be able to deliberate in private against a *background* of informed and open public debate of like cases. Though the public cannot be directly consulted about the particular lie you contemplate telling it may still be indirectly consulted provided that you have access to its reaction to past (or hypothetical) cases that have come to light. The (informed) public's reaction to past cases may then give you useful guidance on how it would react were you able to consult it regarding the lie you have in mind.

The point in consulting public opinion here is not, then, that a consensus for or against lying in certain circumstances settles the qestion of whether it is right or wrong to do so. But on this particular matter of maintaining trust, which is what is at stake when we are contemplating the permissibility of lying, people's actual expectations in various situations are both importantly relevant and, in the absence of debate, obscure. Hence the value and particular relevance of public discussion.

It is only through open discussion of deception in medical practice that we discover the huge discrepancy between the importance attached to truthfulness by patients on the one hand and by doctors and nurses on the other.[21] And only through further more detailed case-related discussion that is both informed and open, including not just any patients but a relevant variety of patients, that we may learn the extent to which there is or could emerge consensus on patients' expectation in various types of situations.

While putting the lie you would tell to this indirect test – matching it up for comparison with what seem to be relevantly similar cases that are being debated – by no means ensures that your judgement on the case in hand will be sound, it may yet be the best available approach, a most useful way of developing what Sissela Bok calls 'a more finely tuned moral sense'.[22] If so, in schools of journalism as in schools of medicine, the examination of cases from an ethical viewpoint is to be encouraged. But, of course, the study of cases need not and indeed should not, be confined to such schools. Members of these schools need to inform their studies by consulting more widely the views of non-members – and above all is such wider, open consultation appropriate where the issues under scrutiny relate to trust.

CONCLUSION

Honesty, I have argued, requires not that you never tell a lie but that you tell a lie only if in the circumstances it is justified. Because of the difficulty of precisely targeting your lies and of the general penumbra of deception that surrounds and sustains their telling, it is not enough to justify a lie to establish that it is aimed at liars or consenters only.

There remain two forms of justification for telling a lie: that your duty not to lie is overridden by another perfect duty more pressing in the circumstances, which makes telling the lie morally obligatory, or that your duty not to lie is overridden by another imperfect duty more pressing in the circumstances, which makes telling the lie morally permissible.

Duties, whether perfect or imperfect, do not fall into any fixed hierarchy. Thus either type of justification requires an examination of particular circumstances. Are we looking at a lie of parent to child – and if so, to a toddler or an adolescent? – about the risks of talking to strangers (is it wrong to exaggerate?) or about the child's genetic parentage? Are we looking at a confidence given to a journalist by a stranger on a train or by an interviewee to whom the journalist has given repeated assurances that nothing will go further without explicit consent (and what if this informant turns out to be malicious and possibly dangerous?) and is the confidence about a public figure or about a public figure's child? Because of the critical relevance of circumstances we benefit by applying the publicity test, by discussing cases in all their specificity. Only through engaging in that form of ethical analysis may journalists and others acquire the competence to judge soundly whether a particular lie is justified.

It may be suggested that investigative journalists who are prepared to lie to get their stories (and the editors who print their stories) are hypocrites, lying in the name of truth.[23] In most instances that is probably true: while our attention here has been so much focused on the rare situation where a lie may be justified, we should not lose sight of the fact that it is overwhelmingly typical for lies to be told in circumstances that do not justify their telling and where it would not even occur to an honest person that a lie might be necessary or permissible. Yet I have sought to show that lying in order to detect and expose lies is not necessarily hypocritical; sometimes it may be morally necessary or permissible for a journalist to lie, and then the journalist's lie will (when revealed) appear justified even to those who are really honest, who genuinely care about truthfulness.

NOTES

1 Stephen Klaidman and Tom L. Beauchamp, *The Virtuous Journalist* (New York, Oxford University Press, 1987), p.30.
2 See H. Eugene Goodwin, *Groping for Ethics in Journalism*, 2nd edn (Ames, IA, Iowa State University Press, 1987), pp. 152–4.
3 See, on this point, Sissela Bok, *Lying: Moral Choice in Public and Private Life* (London, Quartet, 1980), p. 126.
4 ibid., p. 25.
5 ibid., p. 25.
6 ibid., p. 142.
7 See Goodwin, op. cit., p. 133.
8 Philippa Foot, 'Moral Realism and Moral Dilemmas', in Christopher W. Gowans (ed.), *Moral Dilemmas* (New York, Oxford University Press, 1987), p. 254.
9 Bertrand Russell, *A History of Western Philosophy* (London, George Allen & Unwin, 1946), p. 196.
10 G.J. Warnock, *The Object of Morality* (London, Methuen, 1971), p. 12.

11 Charles Fried, *Right and Wrong* (Cambridge, MA, Harvard University Press, 1978), p. 67.
12 ibid., p.55.
13 Diego Gambetta, *Trust* (Oxford, Blackwell, 1988), p. 234.
14 ibid., p. 233.
15 See Bok, op. cit., pp. 92–106.
16 ibid., p.26.
17 See Sissela Bok, *Secrets: On the Ethics of Concealment and Revelation* (Oxford and New York, Oxford University Press, 1984), p. 114.
18 See Goodwin, op. cit., p. 155.
19 See ibid., p. 133 and p. 145.
20 See Bok, *Lying*, p. 95.
21 ibid., p. xvi.
22 ibid., p. 93.
23 See Goodwin, op. cit., p.4 and p. 133. Cf. Richard M. Clurman, *Beyond Malice* (New Brunswick, NJ, Transaction Publishers, 1988), p. 212.

Chapter 8

Objectivity, bias and truth

Andrew Edgar

It may be suggested that certain issues within the ethics of journalism can be explicated through an approach grounded in hermeneutics. My concern is not primarily with the way in which a report is read, but rather with the way in which journalists read the social events before them. If it can be argued that social action is analogous to a text, and therefore that the procedures of the social sciences are analogous to the interpretation of written texts, then if news reports have significant similarities to accounts of research in the social sciences, they may be seen to follow similar procedures in order to interpret social action. Hermeneutic analysis may therefore legitimately be used to highlight the issues involved in distinguishing between good and bad reports. From a hermeneutic perspective it will be argued that objectivity, in the sense of 'correspondence to the object', is inapplicable as a criterion by which reports may be judged. A report must select from the range of possible (and acceptable) interpretations that a social event yields. However, a morally unacceptable bias is intuitively recognisable in certain reports and forms of reporting. In the conclusion I will suggest a resolution of this tension by appealing to the discourse ethics developed by Apel and Habermas.

RICOEUR AND OBJECTIVITY

'Objectivity' may be defined in two different ways. To use Richard Rorty's wording, as 'characterizing the view which would be agreed upon as a result of argument undeflected by irrelevant considerations', and as 'representing things as they really are'.[1] It might be suggested, albeit rather naively, that a morally acceptable news report is one that represents things as they really are. Putting to one side certain complexities, such as questions of privacy, the argument would be that if the propositional content of the report corresponds to events as they actually occurred, and without subjective comment, then while the report could be shocking or boring, it could not be immoral or unjust. In this section it will be argued that such a criterion of morality is not wrong, but is rather inapplicable because it fails to take account of the interpretative procedures inherent to journalism.

In 'The Model of the Text', Paul Ricoeur has used the concept of 'discourse', defined as the event that occurs through the speaker's or writer's use of language, in order to explicate the analogy between the interpretation of a text (in literary hermeneutics) and the interpretation of action (in social science).[2] The procedures of interpretation may be rehearsed.

The unit of the text, for Ricoeur, is the sentence. Interpretation proceeds through a hermeneutic circle, manifest as a movement between part (the sentence) and whole (the text). The meaning of each sentence depends upon the interpretation of the whole text, and vice versa. Ricoeur suggests that this requires the prior presupposition of a certain kind of whole.[3] Prior to reading the whole text, there must be an initial 'guess' as to the structure and meaning of the whole, within which any given sentence may be understood. Gadamer calls this an 'anticipation of meaning' that is itself shaped by the cultural tradition to which the reader belongs.[4] As such, Ricoeur's 'guess' is neither subjective nor arbitrary, but rather grounded in the beliefs and expectations normal to competent members of a given culture. Such beliefs 'bias' our interpretation, through the prejudices (*Vorurteil* – literally 'pre-judgement') that shape our cultural horizon.[5] Yet the hermeneutic circle entails that this anticipation of meaning, and its component beliefs, should continually be tested and modified through the encounter with the details of the text. For Ricoeur the text is a structured totality of sentences, and the purpose of interpretation is to explicate this structure. Each sentence will, more or less consciously, be assessed in terms of its importance in relation to other sentences, and hence in terms of the adequacy of the anticipation of the whole. Ricoeur notes that it 'is always possible to relate the same sentence in different ways to this or that sentence considered as the cornerstone of the text. A specific kind of onesidedness is implied in the act of reading.'[6] The interpretation of a text is, then, never complete or perfect. A text is characterised by its plurivocity, such that it is 'open to several readings and to several constructions'.[7]

In sum, the process of interpretation entails a movement away from the original text. Just as a map that is the same size as its territory is useless, so too is a report that reproduces the original text in its entirety and without further comment. Such a document would not constitute an interpretation. Interpretation involves the selection and ordering of the parts of the text. While one interpretation may claim to be better than others, it cannot claim to be definitive. It is necessarily incomplete, and biased by the horizon within which interpretation occurs.

For Ricoeur this hermeneutic procedure grounds the interpretation of social action. He identifies four characteristics of discourse. These will be rehearsed, albeit not in Ricoeur's order, and their relevance to the hermeneutic procedures inherent within jounalism discussed.

The temporal character of discourse

First, both spoken discourse and social action exist only fleetingly. In order to fit the above model of interpretation each must be capable of being objectified as a text. It is, in both cases, meaning that is fixed in opposition to the fleeting event.[8] Writing transcribes the propositional or locutionary content of spoken discourse. This is not yet an act of interpretation, for transcription is akin to the full-scale map, and further it does not grasp the illocutionary or performative content of the speech event. The meaning of the speech event, as a speech-act, goes beyond the mere words used to the use made of them. The precise words used may therefore be of less significance than the context and way in which they are used. Interpretation must account for and assess the importance of such illocutionary factors.

Speechless acts provide an analogous case, having locutionary as well as illocutionary content. The class of action verbs may be used to fix the action in a text, through predication. The distinctiveness of the locutionary content of an action is not simply that it can be identified and re-identified through an action verb.[9] Rather, the action does not exist as action prior to its propositional formulation. This position is analogous to that of the text. While a physical object, of sound or script, must exist prior to interpretation, it may be suggested that the text as something meaningful does not exist until it is interpreted. So too, in the case of social action, a physical event, that may be termed 'behaviour', must exist prior to its being fixed in a proposition. The event exists as social action only in so far as it has been fixed as meaningful, for such fixing embodies the manner in which the action has been understood by members of society (including the performer). The predication of behaviour as action does not fix the essence of the action, but rather the manner in which actors themselves respond to it.

While this predication corresponds to the transcription of the propositional content of the speech event, unlike transcription it is itself already interpretative. The chronicler is typically confronted by a range of predicates that could be applied to the action. For example, an action could be 'using an axe' or 'chopping wood'. Beyond this, the interpretation is deepened (for Ricoeur to the level of explanation) by relating this act to others, and to the purpose of the action. ('Chopping wood', at an elementary level, becomes 'preparing a fire'.) A series of events is thereby seen to form a structured totality of parts, and thus a text. The meaning of a given act comes to rest upon the end towards which it is seen to be performed.

More precisely, the individual social event is akin to a sentence, not to a text. It is a part, the interpretation of which will depend upon the gradual unfolding of further events, and the projection of conflicting meanings for the greater whole. Habermas gives the following exposition for historical narratives:

> The sentence, 'The Thirty Years War began in 1618', presupposes that at least those events have elapsed that could not have been narrated by any observer at the outbreak of the war. According to the context, the expression 'Thirty Years War' signifies not only a military happening that extended through three decades but the political collapse of the German Empire, the postponement of capitalist development, the end of the Counter-Reformation, the motif for a Wallenstein drama, etc. The predicates with which an event is narratively presented require the appearance of later events in the light of which the event in question appears as an historical event.[10]

To this it may be added that the narrative presentation of a contemporary event, as is typical of journalism, entails a similar choice of predicates. First, the reporting of even a contemporary event entails some temporal distance. Second, the choice of predicates will differ according to the journalist's cultural horizon.

Referential character of discourse

This may be further explicated by reference to Ricoeur's third characteristic of discourse, concerning the structure of reference. Spoken discourse, and by analogy the social event, make ostensive reference to the immediate situation within which they occur.[11] As Ricoeur expresses this in 'The Hermeneutical Function of Distanciation': 'reference is determined by the ability to point to a reality common to the interlocutors'.[12] Written discourse and the meaning of social action, as objectifications of the event, no longer rest upon a situation common to the performer and the interpreter, so that ostensive reference is no longer possible. At an extreme, the terms used in a text relate only to other words and to other texts. However, Ricoeur does not wish to argue that a text is without reference. Through non-ostensive reference the text invokes a 'world' (*Welt*) rather than a situation (*Umwelt*). That is to say that the terms within a text, in their interrelation to other texts, allow the reader to project, in the act of interpretation, a complex symbolic world that could correspond to the text. Gadamer uses this same distinction more boldly, suggesting that the situation is experienced immediately (akin to the habitat to which non-human animals react instinctively). World, conversely, provides humans with 'another attitude towards [the situation], a free, distanced attitude, which is always realised in language'. Language 'is variable, not only in the sense that there are foreign languages that one can learn, but also in itself, in that it contains different possible ways of saying the same thing'.[13]

The hermeneutic circle thereby proceeds through a series of projections of the whole, exploring the adequacy of different ways of saying the same thing. It is thus that the meaning of the social action and the text engage with the horizon of interpretation, such that the interpreter draws on the broad cultural horizon into which they have been socialised in order to transcend the immediacy of the present. Ricoeur writes that to 'understand a text is at the same time to light up our own situation, or, if you will, to interpolate among the predicates of our situation all the significations which make a *Welt* of our *Umwelt*'.[14]

This characteristic would initially appear to be irrelevant to news reporting. A news report has real referents, and a demand for the report to correspond to the object must rest upon this. The news report of a hurricane, be it in Britain or the West Indies, will be a report of something that actually occurred. (It may be noted that a hurricane is a social event in so far as it affects social action.) However, the text of the report is necessarily sundered from the real event. It is a representation of that event to its reader. In reading the report the reader does not experience the complexity or immediacy of the real event. Rather, the text selects from the real complexity, both in terms of the real events highlighted and of the descriptions given to them. For the reader, the events thereby come to exist as meanings fixed in the text. Following Ricoeur's argument, such meanings will be related to other texts and meanings, through the structuring of the report and in the reader's own interpretation. (It may be allowed that such meanings could include individuals' memories of personal experiences.) The use of the term 'hurricane' to describe a storm in Britain facilitates a relationship to texts that describe storms in the West Indies. Further, the term separates this report from normal British weather reports. Hence, even for the person who experienced the original event, and may have interpreted it in terms of a night's lost sleep, the immediate situation is opened up (through the horizon invoked) to a world of global weather disturbances.

A specific journalistic horizon may be identified, through which the journalist interprets reality. This horizon is constituted by the journalist's 'news values', which is to say, by the stock of knowledge and competences, typically taken for granted by the journalist, by which any event may be assessed as being newsworthy. A given event occurs amid a plethora of other social events to which the journalist may or may not respond. The journalist's initial decision to attend to the event will rest upon the anticipation of the place of that event in a broader whole. The whole will in part be constituted as the journalist's perception of 'reality'. The journalist will be aware of past, current and (anticipated) future events that compete for coverage and in relationship to which the given event may be placed as part of a totality. Beyond this, an emphasis may be placed upon the possibilities of predication that the event allows. An event that cannot be filmed is of little importance to a television news programme. Conversely, Braham claims that those events 'which are readily associated with conflict, tension, threat and violence are the most likely to make news'.[15] This may be an oversimplification, but it indicates the importance of dramatic presentation to a popular press. Further, what Ricoeur would term the explanation of the event may tend to be carried out within a limited framework. Explanations of action will be individualistic, and be made with reference to certain taken for granted assumptions concerning the nature of the polity and civil society.

In sum, and against the demand for objectivity, while a report must have a referent in reality, the referent is constituted as meaning only in the text. The importance that the event has to the journalist is related to the pragmatic requirements of journalism and prejudices that take the form of frameworks for interpretation, within which events may be placed. Difficulty in placing an event within such frameworks entails that it will have little or no importance as news. As with all interpretation, a news report does not grasp the event definitively, but within a given horizon. To interpret an event as news does not entail that it corresponds to its interpretation within non-journalistic horizons. Such horizons may give greater or lesser importance to the event, and may describe it in a different (and more or less complex) manner.

The author of discourse

Ricoeur's second characteristic of discourse is the dissociation of the text from the mental intention of the author. While the initial interpretation of any event may appear to be the act of an isolated individual, the process of interpretation has an intersubjective grounding. First, the horizon of interpretation is itself formed in a social tradition. The horizon is learnt by the individual in a continuing process of socialisation. Second, the interpretation of one individual may be challenged or confirmed by any other, not least by bringing a distinct horizon to the event, or a horizon that has been modified by experience of subsequent events. The author of a text (and analogously, the performer of an act) therefore has no privileged position in the process of interpretation. While an actor may attribute meaning to their action, typically through articulating the purpose for which they performed the action, this meaning can be no more definitive than any other. The purpose of the student who shot Arch-Duke Ferdinand was not to start a world war. (Indeed, considering Habermas's remarks above, they did not start a 'world war' until 1939, when the 'Great War' could be reclassified.)

This raises a number of problems. The treatment of the author in contemporary hermeneutics appears to be ethically questionable. The interpretation of a will is carried out in such a way as to reproduce the author's intentions. Yet the author's intentions are disregarded in the interpretation of a literary text. It may further be argued that journalism diverges most markedly from the historical or literary sciences in so far as the performers of the actions that journalism reports are (typically) still alive and able to respond to the journalistic interpretation. Yet, from the interactionist perspective, this is no different from all interactive processes of disputing meaning. The actor may defend his/her interpretation of the action, but with no special privilege over the other participants in the process of interpretation. This is because the consequences of the action (and hence the further social events that the initial action stimulates) go beyond the performer's intentions. In effect, for the student to protest that he/she did not mean to start a war is beside the point, as too would holding him/her responsible for the war's casualties. This is to say that the recognition of both the actor's intentions and the unintended consequences of the action when interpreting the meaning of the action entails a degree of separation of hermeneutic and ethical issues. On the one hand, the author may be held responsible only for the intended consequences of his/her action (for example, shooting an arch-duke, not starting a war). On the other hand, the interpreter cannot arbitrarily attribute meaning to an action. Specifically, it would be wrong, both ethically and as a hermeneutic procedure, to attribute an intention to an actor that cannot be rationally justified, or to confuse the unintended consequences of an action with the actor's intention.

The addressee of discourse

The final characteristic of discourse is the universal range of its addressees. While spoken discourse is addressed to the interlocutors who are present in a situation, written discourse is addressed to whoever knows how to read.[16] The audience constitutes itself, and is beyond the control of the author. Just as the author or speaker loses their privileged position in the text, so too does the initial audience. By analogy, Ricoeur argues, a social action is an 'open work', such that its meaning is open to new references and relevance through the process of its interpretation and reinterpretation.[17] This is a further aspect of the third characteristic. Any person is capable of interpreting an action or text to accord with their horizon, and reciprocally to use the action to challenge their horizon.

This again seems problematic in the case of journalism. It appears to disregard any claims to privacy that an actor or author may make, and thereby to suggest that the journalist need not respect privacy. Such a response, however, fails to recognise the relationship of privacy to the act (or text). Ricoeur does not explicitly address the question of privacy. He possibly blurs the issue by implying that spoken discourse can be directed at a chosen audience. Strictly, the audience of spoken discourse is limited by physical factors (for example, the capacity for sound to carry). The audience must be present in the immediate situation, but the situation cannot be exhaustively defined by the speaker. While the speaker may intend the discourse to be heard only by one person, he/she may be able to do little to prevent it being overheard by others. From this it may be argued that a social event is inherently neither private nor public. Rather, 'private' is a predicate that may be ascribed to the event, in the process of fixing its meaning. The speakers and actors may intend the event to be private, but it ceases to be so if overheard. The eavesdropper may of course concur with the speaker's intention, and not repeat what they have heard. If so, the interpretation of the act as private is restored.

At a superficial level hermeneutics does ignore claims to privacy. Yet it does so because the processes of interpretation are prior to any predication. An action can be private only within a cultural horizon that recognises privacy, and then only in so far as the community accepts the actor's claim to privacy. Hermeneutics will not detail the criteria by which the privacy of a particular case should be judged, yet it would encompass the process of interpretation that resulted in the act being described (and hence its meaning being fixed) as private.

BIAS

Journalism cannot be objective, for that presupposes that an inviolable interpretation of the event as action exists prior to the report. In order to explicate this, the relationship of hermeneutics to journalism may be summarised following Ricoeur's four characteristics of discourse. A news report fixes the meaning of a social event, albeit that the meaning cannot be definitive. (A news report is a moment in a process of interpretation, and the specific interpretation chosen is 'biased' by the horizon of the journalists and readers.) The performers of the reported action have a part to play in the interpretation of the action, but their interpretation is not privileged. The report exists as a text that, in Ricoeur's terms, 'interrupts' the referentiality of the original acts. (The events reported therefore have meaning through the relationship they develop to other texts and meanings.) Finally, in so far as any event may, potentially, be fixed as meaningful and transmitted to others, any event, prima facie, is the legitimate subject matter of journalism.

This might suggest that the limits that are to be placed on journalism are minimal. To criticise a report for distorting reality is incoherent, for the best interpretation must distort reality. The issue may be explored by examining an example of intuitively unacceptable bias.

Carol and Barry Smart[18] argue that the image of rape presented in news reports distorts the reality of rape. They draw initially on Brownmiller's analyis of American news coverage of rape. The rape cases reported in the media are not typical. The distribution of characteristics attributed to the victim (and the assailant) in news reports diverges from that found in official statistics. Reported rapes include a disproportionate number of young, white, middle-class, 'attractive' victims. The Smarts' own analysis of the situation in Britain centres upon the reporting of court cases. Again, a disproportionate number of 'attractive' victims, but also working-class assailants, are reported. The comparison of reports to the court transcripts suggests that the reports are 'selective', first by printing information extracted from the victim, that 'might be argued [to constitute] irrelevant and humiliating material'.[19] Second, the motivation of the rapist is established by the journalists, through reporting statements from the defending counsel and the judge's summing up. 'Rarely . . . is the victim's or the prosecuting counsel's reasoning reported.' This leads to a image of the rapist as motivated by sexual frustration and arousal, and serves to shift responsibility to the woman in terms of her supposedly provocative or irresponsible behaviour prior to the rape. The example of hitch-hiking is highlighted.[20]

In the light of the hermeneutic argument, this comparison of reportage and reality is problematic. First, official statistics are themselves an interpretation of reality. Social statistics (and rape statistics acutely so) are dependent upon processes of social interaction, here involving the victim, police, doctors, etc., through which the meaning of any event is fixed and thereby recorded under the appropriate statistical heading. (While unlikely, it is not inconceivable that there may be systematic reasons for 'attractive' women not to report rape, leading the media, unwittingly and ironically, to redress the imbalance.) The fixing of an event as news is distinct from its fixation in a statistic, and neither can claim the privilege of being a definitive interpretation of 'reality'. Second, for the reporting of court cases, journalists must necessarily 'select' in order to interpret. Thus is the report distinguished from the transcript. The Smarts themselves note that 'press accounts typically select particular statements that are compatible with the specific negotiated outcome of the trial'.[21] Such selection is objectionable only in so far as it omits points of view that dissent from this negotiated outcome. What this entails is that selection omits those views that fall outside the horizon of interpretation adopted by journalists and readers for the interpretation of rape. This horizon may be investigated.

It has been suggested above that the horizon of the journalist is the embodiment of their news values. The coverage of rape highlights the process by which an event is interpreted as news, and further how that event is fixed by a specific form of description (and hence Ricoeur's first characteristic of discourse). Superficially the selection of rape as a newsworthy event may be seen in terms of 'normal news values'. Braham's claim that events readily associated with conflict and violence make news, suggests something of the appeal of rape stories. As the Smarts argue, they involve both crime and sex, thus giving them a dual status to the tabloid press.[22] However, in so far as rape as such is not immediately newsworthy, but rather rape events in which specific characteristics are typically attributed to the victim, a further process of selection occurs. To understand this, and the specific manner in which the events are described, appeal may be made to the third of Ricoeur's characteristics of discourse. The written discourse opens up a world, beyond the immediate situation. In this case, the tabloid report constructs its world through appeal to a broader system of cultural values and texts. For the Smarts, following Brownmiller, this is the culture of male sexual fantasy. The *News of the World* is thereby seen to have a 'novelette style', and rape reports in general are seen to exist as texts in relation to other texts within the newspaper (such as pin-up photographs, advertisements and cartoons) and elsewhere (including novels) that depict women as sexual objects.[23] The journalist's news values may therefore be seen to correspond to a horizon that rests upon a patriarchal cultural tradition.

Ricoeur's other characteristics of discourse may be seen to be reflected in this reportage. The second characteristic, concerning the intentions of the actor, is reflected in the construction of the assailant's motivation, as noted above. A subtle interplay of personal motivation and impersonality occurs. The rapist's own accounts of his action may be cited. The Smarts give the example: 'C. told police he had not had sex for eight months.'[24] As such the interpretation remains individualistic. Yet this is not a self-sufficient explanation of motivation, or expression of intention. It is a mere assertion of a fact that is not related, by necessity, to the rape. Explanation rests upon an explicit or implicit appeal to other explanatory principles. Typically interpretation is worked out in terms of 'natural' sexual drives. (The journalist does not thereby impose his/her own interpretation, but rather draws upon the interpretation that is dominant in the court case, and hence, for example, in the judge's summary.) This interplay does serve to exclude other explanations, such as the political explanations current in the social sciences and feminism.

Ricoeur's fourth characteristic, concerning the universal range of addressees of the event, is reflected in the Smarts' comment that reports print information that 'might be argued [to constitute] irrelevant and humiliating material'.[25] They thereby highlight the possibility of dispute over the privacy of any given element of the event. The fact that the rape has become a court case makes the rape itself, outside reporting restrictions, a public action, addressed to all who wish to attend. The journalist need respect privacy only in so far as it is enshrined in law.

GADAMER AND TRUTH

In the above example the tension between moral intuition and hermeneutic procedure recurs. Specifically, hermeneutics appears to make moral relativism unavoidable, in that a given horizon of interpretation may be unacceptable (here that of patriarchal culture,) but only from another horizon. As such the moral judgements brought, for example, by the Smarts may be criticised in so far as they are valid only from within their own horizon. This appeal to relativism echoes Anderson and Sharrock's criticism of the sociology of the mass media for failing to engage with its own epistemological relativism.[26] They see sociological criticism of news reporting as being grounded not in the sociologist's recognition that a report has distorted reality *per se*, but rather in that the report diverges from the sociologist's way of making sense of reality. The sociologist's claim that their interpretation is definitive is not valid.

An appeal may be made to Gadamer's hermeneutics in order to

challenge these intimations of relativism. While Gadamer's hermeneutics emphasises the importance of the prejudices that constitute all horizons of interpretation, he also raises the possibility of the misunderstanding of a text. Hence, he writes of 'distinguishing the true prejudices, by which we understand, from the false ones by which we misunderstand'.[27] Gadamer's solution to this problem rests upon the analogy that he draws between the hermeneutic circle and a conversation.[28] The structure of the conversation is analysed in the following manner. First, the disputants must not talk at cross purposes. Each disputant must therefore be able to challenge what has just been said, and ask for clarification. Second, the conversation is conducted according to the object with which the disputants are concerned. That is to say, the disputants do not strive to win the argument, but to establish the truth of the topic under discussion. Finally, no disputant can be allowed the power to suppress a question.[29]

The model for such conversation is the Platonic dialogue. At its centre is the question, in that the conversation rests upon the freedom for each of its participants to ask questions of the others. The question itself has a dual structure, in being directed and yet open. The question has direction in so far as it requires a specific answer, and makes this requirement in so far as it is bound by a specific horizon. The question is not then a blind challenge to an opinion, but emerges from the questioner's recognition that there is something, the truth of which they do not know. Conversely the question must be open to different, and indeed opposite answers. As Gadamer expresses this, 'questions include the antithesis of yes and no, of being like this and being like that'.[30] As such, the question opens up the object, placing it in a state of indeterminacy. That which was previously taken for granted is revealed, at least for the moment, as being problematic. False questions lack this structure, by either presupposing an answer or having no specific direction.

The structure of the question is implicit in all experience, in terms of the 'recognition that an object is different and not as we first thought'.[31] This does not entail, simply, that a question must be asked of the object as to what it is, for that is too open a question. Rather, the object itself directs a question at the observer, as to the adequacy of their preconceptions. This is the structure that recurs in hermeneutic experience. Hence, '[f]or an historical text to be made the object of interpretation means that it asks a question of the interpreter'.[32] This is grounded in the initial address that the text makes to the reader. For a text to ask a question, it must say something that is of significance to the reader. A question exposes undetermined possibilities, and as such must pass doubt upon the beliefs of the reader. The process of interpretation is concerned with the 'objective validity' of what a text says.[33] This is to repeat Ricoeur's relationship of event to meaning, albeit within a new context. If Gadamer writes that 'the goal of all communication and understanding is agreement concerning the object',[34] then the object in question is the objectified meaning of the text, 'divorced from the fleeting circumstances of its actuality'.[35] As with conversation, the process of interpretation is led by the validity of the topic of the text. It is neither a reconstruction of the intentions of the original author, nor an absorption of the text to the intentions of the reader.

Yet the conversation is not simply between the text and the reader, but rather between their respective horizons of interpretation. If questions are raised, then each has construed the meaning of the object differently. Such construction rests upon the prejudices brought to bear in the projection of meaning. This entails that what is at stake in interpretation is the *Welt*, the possible projections of meaning, rather than anything immediately experienced within the *Umwelt*. If the process of interpretation is one that serves to challenge the claims to truth made by the text and by the reader, then such claims do not centre upon particular issues, but upon the prejudices that constitute the disputants' respective horizons. In so far as a text fails to correspond to the meaning that the reader attributes to it in anticipation, it acts as a stimulus to the reader to question (and indeed to recognise) their prejudice. Gadamer may therefore claim that the hermeneutician 'is not able to separate in advance the productive prejudices that make understanding possible from the prejudices that hinder understanding and lead to misunderstandings'. This separation rather takes place as understanding itself.[36]

If journalism is a hermeneutic process, albeit typically directed at events rather than texts, then it may be suggested that Gadamer's questioning of prejudice ought to be inherent to it. This would entail that the prejudices which the journalist brings to bear upon a given event can potentially be questioned by the event itself. This needs further explication in terms of the analogy of the text and society. The event is but a part of the social totality. The bounds of totality of text and society are not self-evident. On the one hand, the interpretation of a text is not necessarily exhausted by the immediate document. Interpretation, as Ricoeur's analysis of non-ostensive reference demonstrates, requires appeal to other texts. On the one hand, the selection of particular events as relevant to the understanding of a given event is dependent upon interpretative procedures. Different interpretations will make appeal to different totalities. This does not entail a distortion of the interpretation, but rather a potential enrichment. Crucially, the interpreter must be open to the challenge that an event, however remote it seems from the centre of the totality, can provide to the existing interpretation.

It was suggested above that the news values which constitute the journalist's horizon of interpretation include explanatory frameworks. Events are related to each other, through more or less sophisticated models of social institutions and psychological structures. As such they serve to define a relevant totality. As with all prejudices, news values are therefore selective. It is, however, the nature of this selectivity that is of importance. The logic of question and answer is not always obviously present. The 'newsworthy' rape, for example, is itself selected from among rapes. Hence, a criterion that is alien to the event, and thus to the meaning and truth of the event, is imposed upon it. Metaphorically, the event is employed to support a single protagonist's argument. Events that may question the stereotype are excluded, their questions suppressed. This exclusion extends to those events that may provide radical explanations of rape. Description and explanation alike are conducted within the *Welt* of male fantasy.

Gadamer's metaphorical conversation entails an encounter between horizons. While the journalist's horizon is evident, that of his/her opponent is less so. For the event (or sequence of events) to be analogous to the text, it must bear its own horizon. This is the case in so far as the actors who perform the event have their own interpretations of it. The actors, like the author, are not thereby given privileges. Interpretation does not try to reconstruct their original intentions. Rather, as with Gadamer's textual hermeneutics, it engages with the validity of these intentions, attempting to reconstruct the question which they seek to answer. The actors' interpretations, however, need not cohere into a single horizon. Indeed, in conflicts horizons will be antagonistic. The interpretation of an event may involve other disputants, and hence further horizons. An assault may involve the companions of both parties, police, counsellors, lawyers, social scientists, and so on. The 'conversation' within which journalists participate is not, therefore, metaphorical. As the Smarts make clear, reporting is part of a political process that serves to define rape (and thereby to control the position of women in society).[37]

This recognition of the reality of the debate over the interpretation of social events takes us beyond the limits of Gadamer's hermeneutics. Gadamer's analysis is weak as to the source of questions. He suggests merely an analogy to 'sudden ideas'.[38] His model of interpretation, at this point, is monological. The metaphorical conversation occurs within the individual interpreter's mind. If this were the case with journalism, only the most exceptional journalist (akin to the gifted hermeneutician) could be expected to recognise a radical question posed by a distant event. The intersubjective reality of the interpretation of events, as opposed to texts, makes this apology problematic. Questions are continually being posed by other protagonists. It may then be suggested that false prejudices within the journalistic horizon serve, not merely to avoid alien events, but to remove the legitimacy from oppositional disputants. The reproduction of the patriarchal horizon within rape reporting serves to make alternative horizons (and the interpretations they ground) meaningless. The Smarts note that one element of the horizon of male fantasy is to eliminate the antagonism inherent in rape, by portraying women as wanting or enjoying rape. Shifting responsibility to the victim in court judgments extends this principle. The woman's 'No' is transformed, by the false question, into a 'Yes'.[39]

The relativism inherent in hermeneutics may now be overcome, and hence also journalism's defence of not being social science. The criticism of false prejudice does not rest upon an appeal to the standards and norms of another horizon, nor yet to the object prior to interpretation. Rather, 'objectivity' may be construed in the first of Rorty's senses, as 'characterizing the view which would be agreed upon as a result of argument undeflected by irrelevant considerations'. The discourse ethics developed by Apel and Habermas builds upon Gadamer's hermeneutics by recognising the real, as opposed to the metaphorical, nature of conversation in understanding. The structure of conversation, as analysed by Gadamer, corresponds closely to the 'ideal speech situation' that Apel and Habermas posit as grounding the possibility of all human interaction (however distorted its reality may be). For Apel 'all meaningful human actions and physical expressions . . . involve "claims" . . . and hence can be regarded as potential arguments'.[40] This coheres with the above analyses, in so far as social actions have the structure of questions.

News reports, as interpretations of social action, raise truth claims. The apology that they are 'news' and not 'science' is irrelevant. While the journalist's interpretation of reality is inevitable 'biased' (in Gadamer's sense) it must remain genuinely open to the questions that other actors can pose to it, and as such open to rational argument. Journalism denies its own claim to truth when it forestalls rational argument through strategies that undermine the legitimacy of relevant disputants.

NOTES

1 R. Rorty, *Philosophy and the Mirror of Nature* (Oxford, Blackwell, 1980), pp. 333–4.
2 P. Ricoeur, *Hermeneutics and the Human Sciences*, trans. J.B. Thompson (Cambridge, Cambridge University Press, 1981).
3 ibid., p. 211.
4 H.G. Gadamer, *Truth and Method*, trans. W. Glen-Doepel (London, Sheed & Ward, 1975), p. 261.
5 Gadamer, op. cit., p. 272.
6 Ricoeur, op. cit., p. 212.
7 ibid.
8 ibid., p. 199.
9 ibid., p. 204.
10 J. Habermas, 'A Review of Gadamer's *Truth and Method*', in F. Dallmayr and T. McCarthy (eds), *Understanding Social Inquiry* (Notre Dame, IN, Notre Dame Press, 1977), p. 346.
11 Ricoeur, op. cit., p. 201.
12 ibid., p. 141.
13 Gadamer, op. cit., p. 403.
14 Ricoeur, op. cit., p. 202.
15 P. Braham, 'How the Media Report Race', in M. Gurevitch, T. Bennett, J. Curran and J. Woollacott (eds) *Culture, Society and the Media* (London, Methuen, 1982), pp. 274–5.
16 Ricoeur, op. cit., p. 202.
17 ibid., p. 208.
18 C. Smart and B. Smart, 'Accounting for Rape: Reality and Myth in Press Reporting', in C. Smart and B. Smart (eds), *Women, Sexuality and Social Control* (London, Routledge & Kegan Paul, 1978), pp. 87–103.
19 ibid., p. 98.
20 ibid., pp. 101–2.
21 ibid., p. 98
23 ibid., p. 97.
23 ibid.
24 ibid., p. 98.
25 ibid.
26 D. Anderson and W. Sharrock, 'Biasing the News: Technical Issues in "Media Studies"', *Sociology*, 13 (1979), pp. 367–85.

27 Gadamer, op. cit., p. 266.
28 ibid., p. 260.
29 ibid., p. 330.
30 ibid., p. 328.
31 ibid., p. 325.
32 ibid., p. 333.
33 ibid., p. 260.
34 ibid.
35 ibid., p. 265.
36 ibid., p. 263.
37 Smart and Smart, op. cit., pp. 100f.
38 Gadamer, op. cit., p. 329.
39 See Smart and Smart, op. cit., p. 95.
40 K. O. Apel, *Towards a Transformation of Philosophy*, trans. G. Adey and D. Frisby (London, Routledge & Kegan Paul, 1980), p. 259.

Chapter 9

Women and the press

Teresa Stratford

Given current patterns of media ownership in the UK, women's near invisibility in the controlling positions of our national press should come as no surprise. Our newspapers are run like old boys' clubs, and the recent successes of Wendy Henry (ex-editor of the *People*) and Eve Pollard (editor of the *Mail on Sunday*) have done nothing to change the situation. They wanted the jobs; they therefore played by the rules in order to get them. The rules were not changed to facilitate the progress of other female journalists after them. Long hours, drinks with the boys and a disregard for childcare (no workplace nurseries here) remain the norm.

There is an interesting parallel with the careers of Conservative MPs like Edwina Currie, and most significantly Margaret Thatcher. Entry into the club is possible for women, as long as no attempt is made to alter or even question the status quo. Our national newspapers, like the Houses of Lords and Commons, are deeply conservative institutions. Their ownership by rich, white middle-aged men, and their editorship usually by the same type of men, explain the difficulties they have in reflecting recent changes in society in any but the most stereotypical ways. The *Guardian* and *The Independent* try harder than most, and the *Daily Mail* and the *Daily Express* deal with social issues by special sections and features. Thus we have 'Guardian Women' and 'Femail' covering issues like divorce, childcare, health care, adoption and fertility problems, as if these matters only affected half the population. It is an absurdity, of course, but it reflects the discomfort felt by the men who control our press when they have to consider issues which do not necessarily belong to the conventional political or economic spheres.

There have been numerous complaints against British newspapers about various representations of women, especially, but not by any means exclusively, against tabloid newspapers. There have been some famous and successful court cases. Carmen Proetta's case against *The Sunday Times* in 1988 is very well known.[1] Esther Rantzen's case against the *People* is another example, significant for preserving her reputation as a woman whom children can trust – vital for her role in Child-line.[2] Common to almost all complaints is the grievance that the woman's character and personal life has been caricatured by the newspaper concerned, with no regard to personal suffering but, it seems, great regard to selling newspapers.

The caricature and sensationalisation of women's lives in the press is clearly an effective selling point: the *Sun* and the *Daily Mirror* are Britain's most popular newspapers. Both papers have found that nothing sells like a scandal, especially if it can be a sex scandal, and more serious papers have borrowed their techniques. Despite promoting their papers as daring and *risqué*, however, tabloid editors and owners are distinctly uncomfortable with issues of sex and sexuality; only by sensationalising and caricaturing such issues can they deal with them. Two illustrative studies are included below, to look at what they do and why they do it in some detail. The first, on Page 3 Girls, is included because the notion of placing a nearly naked young woman on a newspaper page has nothing to do with news coverage but a great deal to do with newspaper circulation. So many women find it unacceptable that its continued existence is probably the clearest sign there is of newspaper owners' and editors' contempt for women's views. The second study discusses representations of sexuality, particularly where lesbians are concerned; this must be the most uncomfortable area of all for journalists and editors to cover.

'SHE'S ON PAGE 3'

Photographs of topless young women are a fairly recent newspaper feature. The *Sun* started the practice, to be followed in the bid for increased readership by the *Daily Star* and the *Daily Mirror*. The *Mirror* later changed its policy to featuring women wearing swimsuits or underwear; no longer topless. They were originally sold to the public as a daring and *risqué* venture; indeed tabloid editors still try to maintain a saucy air about their publications and, along with gossip pages and features on pop stars, Page 3 Girls are supposed to contribute to this. Women who criticise papers for featuring Page 3 Girls are therefore, by contrast, boring, dowdy prudes – and probably secretly jealous of the girls' wonderful figures.

No one has felt this more than Clare Short. Following her introduction of 'the Page Three Bill',[3] she was subject to repeated insults by a tabloid press whose overreaction can only have been a sign of panic. As well as many references to her physical appearance ('The buxom Ms Short', for example), the *Sun* suggested that she was not even quite sane, with its 'Crazy Clare' campaign. Unfortunately, she was met with a similar verbal reaction when she presented the bill in the House of Commons, from male Tory MPs unable to conceal their alarm that the status quo was being questioned in their own chamber.

In fact, the bill made some progress on both occasions that Clare Short introduced it; its failure to become law was due to lack of committee time, not lack of support (and over 3,000 letters written to Ms Short about it attest to the support she had among the electorate). It is a pity that its progress was halted in this way, for it is an elegant bill; it avoids censorship completely by redefining what a newspaper is – that is, a newspaper cannot by definition be a publication which features naked or nearly naked women or men. It therefore highlights the anomalous position occupied by the tabloid press: full of uncertain gossip and anecdotes about television characters, they none the less include just enough news to avoid being dismissed as total fiction, but only just, and the *Sport* has abandoned all claims to news reportage; its sales are based on the popularity of items which no one relies on as true, and newsagents can be excused for not knowing where in the shop to place it (although many would say the bin would not be a bad idea).

Conservative MPs jeering at Clare Short looked ridiculous, but they were right to be alarmed at her move. For Page 3 Girls, far from being a daring venture, have become an institution, one on which the Tory tabloids are heavily dependent. Like the politics of the *Sun* and the *Star*, they indicate acceptance of the status quo: women's place is the bedroom, not the boadroom, and women's minds should be on their figures, not politics. The *Daily Mirror's* use of the same tactic belongs to old-style, right-wing Labourism, conducted by men in smokey pubs. Questioning Page 3 is indeed challenging, and of course while it remains, there is a daily reminder of sex-role stereotyping at its worst in the media.

Tabloid journalists and editors respond to criticism of Page 3 by pointing out that no woman is coerced into it. There are more applicants to be Page 3 Girls than the papers can possibly use, even with a different young woman each day. It's true, and it is instructive to see where all these hopeful models come from.

Class is central to the Page 3 issue. Middle-class people tend not to read the *Sun* or the *Star*. Middle-class girls tend not to dream about appearing on Page 3. They have no need; most of them have job prospects which promise more interest, more respect and a longer career elsewhere. It is no accident that most Page 3 Girls come from working-class homes. As photographer Harry Ormesher has pointed out, 'Unemployment is the biggest factor. A young girl with a nice body can be led to believe her charms can get her off the dole queue.'[4] What would the alternative be for those girls?

It is evidently a question asked by their parents too. Far from hiding her topless modelling from her mother, a Page 3 Girl is likely to have been groomed and prepared for the assignment by her, according to Yvonne Paul, who runs a model agency.[5] There is considerable outlay for a woman wishing to do this kind of work: outfits have to be bought and a portfolio of photographs must be paid for before an agency will even sign her on. This means considerable sacrifice for a working-class family; the hope is always that the young woman will become as successful as Samantha Fox, who was cannily managed by her father, Pat Fox, and now earns enough money from her investment projects not to have to model again. It is a short career, that of the Page 3 Girl.

Samantha Fox became a personality, but most do not. They are not there because they are interesting; rather they are there to represent female sexuality in an attractive and non-threatening way. The Page 3 Girl's biographical details are irrelevant because she is not there as an individual. Friendly, approachable, smiling (always), she has a child's fresh, open face, but a mother's large, nurturing breasts. Her body is coded as sexually available, and if the description of her below reminds you of eating ('tasty Tracey Elvik', 'luscious Linda Lusardi') it is because she is, indeed, an item for consumption. It is this aspect of the Page 3 phenomenon which women find most demeaning, and it is so far from the realities of most women's lives to be anachronistic, a comforting habit retained by the men who run the newspapers to remind themselves daily that the power balance still lies in their favour.

RELATIONSHIPS WITHOUT MEN

Sociologists estimate that up to 10 per cent of the population in the UK is homosexual. The national press, however, uniformly treats heterosexuality as the norm. Invisibility is therefore something with which gay people have to learn to contend in the media. Since even when they do refer to gay people journalists tend to mean male gays, lesbians are doubly invisible.

Given the vocabulary frequently used by journalists to describe them, though, lesbians may well prefer invisibility. Phrases such as 'self-confessed lesbian', 'engaged in homosexual activity' and 'homosexual tendencies' evoke images of people doing shameful things in dark corners. The absence of reference to lesbians in legal rulings on ages of consent suggests that politicians have been as unable as journalists to treat this kind of relationship with the same kind of open discussion as heterosexual relationships.

Lesbianism is therefore generally treated in one of two ways: either as a sad failure on the part of the women concerned (this was the way Julie Goodyear – Bet Lynch of *Coronation Street* – was treated when she spoke about her relationship with Janet Ross); or, predictably, as a juicy scandal which will sell papers. Attempts are often made in the latter case to involve ('implicate') famous entertainers or sportswomen, like Whitney Houston and Joan Armatrading.

One woman who was prepared to talk about her sexual orientation (surely her private business in any case), was Martina Navratilova, whose close relationship with Judy Nelson was discussed by tabloids and more heavyweight newspapers alike. For some time, an attempt was made to compare her unfavourably with the evidently heterosexual Chris Evert, an attempt which foundered because Ms Evert, to her credit, would have none of it.

The same kind of innuendo is used to suggest that famous men are gay (it has been done repeatedly to Cliff Richard and Elton John). Indeed, AIDS has added a new and dramatic angle to reportage of homosexuality. While permitting right-wing Conservatives to put their homophobic ideas into print, it has also created an anomaly of sympathy, which the case of Freddie Mercury illustrates very well: Mr Mercury's lifestyle was of the type which meets with popular disapproval, yet his passing has been mourned to such an extent that the BBC and ITV featured commemorative programmes of him, and all the national daily papers included obituaries of him.

Perhaps it is a sign of lesbians' invisibility that there has been so little media focus on the comparative safety of their sexual activities where AIDS is concerned. But maybe the less focus on private activity the better; there is enough suggestion as it is in the popular press that this very personal aspect of people's lives is the most defining one. While the political stance taken by some people (Peter Tatchell, for example, and the Outrage group), is deliberate many gay people, women and men, may very well prefer to be defined by what they do at work, or which ethnic group they belong to.

In the past the imputation of being lesbian, or of supporting lesbians, has been used as a malicious smear by right-wing daily papers, notably the *Daily Mail* and the *Daily Express* in their coverage of the Greenham Common Peace Camp and the Greater London Council. This kind of reporting really shows how desperate journalists can be, but of course it is harmful both to lesbians and to the institutions thus attacked.

While a calm and reasonable approach to discussing lesbians is certainly to be hoped for, it must be admitted that the current difficulties most tabloids have in reporting situations which do not conform to the editors' ideas of normal (a heterosexual couple) make the prospect seem unlikely without a change in editorial and journalistic direction. There is all too often the suggestion of disease (there is something 'sick' about being a lesbian) as a way of explaining women who prefer to make their intimate relationships without men.

CONCLUSION

Although journalists, like advertisers, claim to be reflecting the attitudes of society rather than shaping them, recent national trends indicate that, with respect to women's lives, they lag behind dismally. Few sections of any of the national papers give the impression of the very powerful changes which society has experienced in recent years. Women are entering the traditionally male professions in large numbers (for example, half of all medical students accepted for training last year were women), and they are running succesful businesses. Much as the media attention given to women like Helena Kennedy and Anita Roddick is deserved, therefore, describing them as exceptions to their gender is no longer appropriate. As inappropriate is the assumption, which is found in *The Independent*, regrettably, as well as in the *Sun*, the *Star*, the *Mirror* and all, that a woman's appearance is the personal characteristic which really matters, and needs to be the primary focus of her attention. Women have always had to work too hard for this to have been the case for any but a privileged few, and nowadays, with so many families being supported and headed by women (one-third of marriages in the UK currently end in divorce) this is truer than ever.

There are excellent guidelines to help journalists avoid sexist stereotyping, produced by the National Union of Journalists (NUJ). They illustrate how, with a little diligence applied even at the level of vocabulary (as basic as 'chair' instead of 'chairman'), a completely different impression can be given. While adoption of the NUJ guidelines is strongly recommended to journalists, so is a change in focus of subject matter, and this applies to heavier papers and tabloids alike. Of course politics, economics and commerce are women's concerns – and health, family matters and relationships are men's. None of these subjects is gender-specific, and as society changes and develops, so should modern journalism. For what is happening is exciting and interesting – and journalism has a part to play in stimulating change and leading debate. A few journalists are doing so – Beatrix Campbell and John Pilger, to name two prominent examples – but most journalists could make much more of the opportunity they have to be a part of the changes, even to influence them, and central to their present inability to do so is the discomfort so many of them show in relation to women and women's roles.

NOTES

1 Carmen Proetta, a witness to the controversial shootings in Gibraltar of three Irish people suspected as being members of the IRA, sued *The Sunday Times* for defamation of character after a report which contained unfounded scurrilous allegations about her.
2 The *People* alleged that Ms Rantzen protected a child sex abuser. Her £250,000 damages were donated to children's charities (in 1991).
3 First introduced into the House of Commons in 1986, then again eighteen months later.
4 Quoted in the *Sunday Mirror*, 8 July 1986.
5 ibid.

Chapter 10

The oxygen of publicity: terrorism and reporting restrictions

Paul Gilbert

SECRECY AND SUFFERING

At one time rulers used to cut out seditious critics' tongues. Now they merely deny them airtime – the 'oxygen of publicity'[1] – for their subversive opinions. But if the critics clamour for the violent overthrow of their rulers might it not be *right* to silence them? If they support terrorism might it not be *right* to deny them airtime?

On 19 October 1988 the United Kingdom Home Secretary banned the broadcasting of utterances by the representatives or supporters of terrorist or pro-terrorist organisations in Northern Ireland (including the legal political party, Sinn Fein). The ban has been widely criticised as infringing the alleged right to freedom of opinion and expression, enshrined, for example, in the United Nations Universal Declaration of Human Rights and the European Convention for the Protection of Human Rights.[2] Yet it has survived legal challenges all the way to the House of Lords, being found a not unreasonable use of the Home Secretary's powers to restrict broadcasting in the national interest.

'In a war,' said Mrs Thatcher at the time, 'you have to suspend some of your civil liberties.'[3] The war she was referring to is, presumably, a war against the IRA, which sees itself as fighting to liberate the Six Counties of Northern Ireland from British control. The implications of this description of a response to terrorism as *war* is something to which we shall return. Meanwhile we need to ask what restrictions on freedom of opinion and expression a war against terrorists might justify. Pre-eminently, of course, it would justify a degree of *secrecy* with respect to military operations. In any war all governments impose restrictions on the reporting of the dispositions, movements and engagements, not only of their own troops, but of those of the enemy, in order to conceal the extent of their information. The reasons for such secrecy may be purely military: to maximise the chances of achieving victory by surprising the enemy. It is only the reporting of military operations themselves which might prejudice this. The reporting of opinions about the war could not, or rather it could only if these opinions concerned what military operations were involved.

Secrecy with respect to military operations is achieved in two ways, by the control of information available in the first place only to government, and by censorship. The extent to which either of these is justified in war is a matter of debate. But, since both methods are in question, this debate turns on the balance between State secrecy and the public's alleged 'right to know', rather than on that between enforced secrecy and freedom of expression. Whatever the extent of a public *right* to know, it is evident that it is often in the interests of people in a war zone to know enough about it to take effective precautions. The peculiarly covert character of military operations against terrorists undoubtedly exposes citizens to risks over and above the ordinary hazards of guerrilla warfare: they are, for example, caught in the crossfire following 'stakeouts', which are of necessity unpublicised. Similarly the reluctance of the authorities to countenance large-scale disruption of ordinary life and thereby concede the effectiveness of terrorist threats has sometimes led them to refrain from passing on warnings of bombs, with fatal consequences for citizens.

In both cases it is the special nature of what is termed 'terrorism' which creates problems in squaring the effectiveness of counter-terrorist operations with the openness about them which would safeguard citizens. For while politicians may sometimes describe their counter-terrorist campaigns as war, they are not, ostensibly, conducted like wars. Ostensibly troops act in support of the civil power to prevent the crime or to detain the criminals involved in terrorist activities. In this situation an assumption must be made which potentially imperils citizens: that terrorists must be pursued and brought to justice, rather than simply contained or rendered ineffective. Although there is no sharp distinction to be drawn between terrorism and guerrilla war, the response to terrorism differs in this respect from that made in a guerrilla war. Counter-terrorist operations display an overtly *non-military* character, since any *military* tactics must, as such, be concealed. But this hampers the kind of disclosure which is made compatibly with military secrecy to safeguard ordinary citizens caught up in open war.

It is, then, not military necessity but political expediency which prevents an overtly military response that principally fosters restrictions on the reporting of terrorist and counter-terrorist incidents. As in open war, however, the preservation of morale and the erosion of the enemy's will to fight are motives for concealment or deception. In times of terrorism there is an additional but related motive. It is to maintain the impression – which may be illusory – that the life of citizens continues more or less normally. That government counter-terrorist tactics are merely policing operations is an essential aspect of this picture. The impression is maintained as long as possible in order to prevent citizens, or outside observers, from suspecting the breakdown of normal government control of its territory, with a consequent loss of morale among its own supporters and a boost to the confidence of its antagonists.

It is common – in cases where, on the one hand, terrorism is successful enough to shade into guerrilla war, or, on the other, popular enough to evoke sympathetic rioting – to suppress any reporting of incidents across an entire area, whether by the exclusion of journalists or by censorship of their reports. In this situation two crucial kinds of fact can be concealed: the *territorial* gains of terrorists, that is their power to hold and administer an area, if only for a period, and, correlatively, the essentially *military* response of government, its use of 'shoot to kill' rather than policing methods. What can also be concealed by such restrictions is *State terrorism*. Indeed there is a natural tendency for an ostensibly civil response to terrorism to become terroristic itself as it resorts to undercover military tactics. Then neither the rule of law nor the rules of war can be expected to constrain government forces, for the former has been exceeded and the latter need not be applied in the absence of any acknowledgement of open conflict, while such an acknowledgement is incompatible with the impression of control which the government seeks to preserve.

Although the political advantage to a government from this sort of reporting restriction may be great, its potential for causing harm is considerable. Ordinary citizens, especially if they are sympathetic to the terrorists' cause, may be subjected to State repression which is thereby shielded from adverse publicity. They may also suffer from the unintended effects of living in an area of conflict, not only as the casualties of attacks directed at others but as victims of hunger, disease and the other hardships of war. Reporting restrictions militate against the relief of their suffering, which may itself be deliberately concealed by government as unwelcome evidence of its failure to secure full control of its territory.

The common excuse of governments for restricting reports of terrorist incidents which command a measure of support or sympathy from some sections of the population is that the reports can induce further public disorder. What may look at first sight like a mere propaganda exercise is presented as conducive to the public good. Doubtless in some cases the disorder arising from imitative violence will be very great. Weighing the benefits and disbenefits of such policies along utilitarian lines is, however, notoriously difficult and uncertain. In this instance there is an additional problem, namely that the success or otherwise of the policy, when it is implemented, in conducing to the public good is something that only government can be in a position to judge, since it alone has access to the necessary information of which others are deprived precisely by the operation of the policy. It is hard to see how a policy which has this consequence can, in general, be to the public good. The temptation to substitute the sectional interest of a particular government for that of the public at large is too strong when the success of the policy is not open to public scrutiny. If a government succumbs to this temptation then no honest utilitarian calculation will be possible as to the public good.

This argument can be generalised. It applies not only to balancing the risks of spreading disorder against the dangers of repression or neglect, but to balancing the loss of any advantage to the State against possible harm to a section of its population. Here we should notice at once that it is not the *public* good, as the utilitarian conceives it, that government considers, but the *national* interest. Yet the government's duty to consider only the national interest is in fact not different in kind from the temptation for it to consider only sectional interests. In neither case are the interests of people in general under consideration. This point is particularly pertinent to situations in which there is a terrorist threat. For these situations are most commonly those in which the official State view of what constitutes the nation is under challenge from the terrorists. In these circumstances what is to the good of the nation as the State conceives it, and what is to the good of the nation which the terrorist recognises, may well differ. The terrorist will view government restrictions on reporting terrorism simply as seeking to preserve the existing national order in order to benefit its present population. In the process a putatively national minority may well be caused to suffer. But no utilitarian calculation has been made with respect to the benefits to people in general, rather than to the State's present population, that might outweigh the minority's suffering.

THE ARGUMENT FROM DEMOCRACY

The foregoing argument evidently applies not only to the justification for restricting reports of terrorist *incidents*, but also to that offered for restricting dissemination of terrorist *opinions*. Of the four considerations reported[4] to have influenced the British Home Secretary in his decision to ban the broadcasting of live interviews with supporters of terrorism it is the fact that such interviews give terrorists publicity deemed contrary to the 'public interest' which is especially relevant here. By the 'public interest' the Home Secretary must have in mind the *national* interest, an interest in preserving British rule in Northern Ireland which is challenged by the IRA. Publicity for those who threaten it with force calls its continuance into question. In this connection even the ban's apparent evenhandedness in being directed at Loyalist as well as Irish Nationalist terrorist groups is significant. For the existence of pro-State terrorist groups is itself an indication of the extent of the threat to the status quo from Nationalist terrorism which the Government is anxious to under-play. It is for this reason that the publicity given to terrorists is described as 'undeserved' – it is undeserved in relation to the Government's official view of the solidity of the Northern Irish settlement.

The Home Secretary's Broadcasting Ban was challenged through the courts by a group of journalists. One of their arguments was that the ban contravened the duty laid upon broadcasters by law to observe 'due impartiality'. Although the argument was rejected by the judges it is an interesting one. It indicates the view that journalists take of their own duties, which some see as conflicting with the aims of the ban. The supposed fact that publicity for the advocates of violence in pursuit of a united Ireland works against the British national interest seems to journalists irrelevant to their duty to present an impartial picture of the present situation and of its possible resolution. So far as presenting an impartial picture of the situation is concerned the objection to reporting restrictions must be that they tend to distort the truth. The suppressing of certain *facts* in the national interest will not enable those who report the facts to give an *accurate* account – although the resulting account will not necessarily be a *partial* (i.e., a biased) one. The suppression of certain *opinions* as to the facts may lead to *inaccuracy*, and must lead to *partiality* (to bias).

The general relation between the journalist's job of uncovering the truth about current affairs and the government's of 'news management' is complex and problematic. What concerns us here is the specific relation between the journalist's role as an impartial reporter of views and a government's restrictions, imposed in the national interest, on the reporting of some views – in the case of the Broadcasting Ban by preventing broadcasts of their holders' voices. A situation analogous to the terrorist case arises in open war. The governments of both sides express views as to the progress of the war and each expects its own news media to give special emphasis to its views in the national interest. Is there a countervailing duty of impartiality here? Or is there, perhaps, a duty which may be overridden by an obligation to protect the national interest?

It is hard to see how to resolve this question in general terms. Radio and television or the press are made up of particular institutions with their own aims and responsibilities. The BBC, for example, is a public corporation which, though ostensibly impartial as between the major political contenders for government, is not expected to be impartial as between a British and a foreign government on any point affecting the national interest. Journalists, whatever their aspirations to independence, are employed by such institutions or produce material for sale to them. The truth may not be what is required. Nor is it possible to imagine a journalistic context in which the truth for its own sake is all that is required. For the point of revealing the truth cannot be divorced from the political impact of doing so, and the impact will need to be assessed prior to publication.

That said, it is one thing to have regard to the national interest in publishing facts or opinions, it is quite another to be prevented by legal constraints from publishing material claimed to be contrary to it, where this does not fall within the limits of that proscribed for reasons of national security. The enforced dissemination of an official version of the facts, brought about by the suppression of other views, does run counter to the supposed role of the news media in a democratic society. In a democracy, the argument runs,[5] voters need to be able to judge the success of government policies, and to do so they must have before them anything relevant to establishing it, not just the government's own rose-tinted version of the relevant facts. For a government to impose its own version is therefore for it to interfere in the democratic process with the aim of remaining in power longer than it might if voters had had at their disposal different versions of the facts. Politically naive as this 'Argument from Democracy' may be, it has the merit of locating press freedom within a framework of political choice. In its application to the reporting of the opinions of terrorist groups, however, it may appear to encounter difficulties. The terrorist's criticisms (for example, of government counter-terrorism), it may be argued, are not those of a group contending for political power within the democratic process. As such they are not pertinent to the political choices of voters, and therefore need not be accorded freedom of expression. This argument is without force. So far as opinions as to the relevant *facts* of the situation are concerned the *origin* of the opinions is not relevant to their value in establishing the truth, which is all the voter seeks to know.

There is, though, a further complication. In order to discover the truth about the situation and to assess government policy the voter will need to know the opinions of the protagonists on how it ought to be resolved. But, whereas the origin of opinions on the facts of the situation is irrelevant to their admissibility, the origin of opinions as to its proper outcome may not be similarly irrelevant. For these opinions enunciate policy options, and here it can be argued that only those that originate from parties involved in the democratic pursuit of power are pertinent to the voter's political choices. Others might then be suppressed as not protected by the Argument from Democracy. The knock-on effect of their suppression would be, however, to deprive voters of information relevant to their assessment of the *facts*, for while the policy opinions themselves might not be able to affect their choice, *that* others hold them might well do so. If this is so then these opinions too should be afforded freedom of expression under the Argument from Democracy.

This is a complex line of reasoning which raises many questions, pre-eminently that of the admissibility to the news media of policy opinions pursued 'undemocratically'; to this we shall return in the next section. What we should now observe is that the line of reasoning need not be taken to expose any incoherence in the Argument from Democracy. That argument attempts to identify certain *illegitimate* restrictions on the news media. It does not seek to identify what restrictions *are* legitimate. As a result a proponent of the argument can reason that if the voter needs information which can only be obtained by the dissemination of a policy opinion, then, however abhorrent that opinion is, it must be disseminated. Perhaps few would wish to follow down this path, which could license the dissemination of, for example, offensive and inflammatory racist policy opinions. The difficulty is to see how to redraw the Argument from Democracy in order to close it off. It could be argued that reports of the holding of the opinon, though not its actual expression, would fit the bill, by giving voters the information they need while not exposing them to undemocratic influences. If this is so then the form of the Broadcasting Ban is entirely apt for its purpose. We shall, however, have reason to question it.

ILLEGITIMATE OPINIONS

The presumption of the Argument from Democracy, that the rights of citizens to consider alternative viewpoints do not stop with their rights as voters to consider the policies of the parties involved in a democratic contest for power, is open to challenge. For, it may be contended, their right to hear viewpoints which take for granted the nature of their national interest does not exhaust their rights as citizens.

We can best consider this claim by examining another of the factors reported to have influenced the imposition of the Broadcasting Ban, namely that television broadcasts by supporters of terrorism create the false impression that such support is itself a *legitimate* political opinion. The common view that support for terrorism is not a legitimate political opinion may be understood to mean that it is not admissible to political debate and hence not tenable as a *political* opinion. The view seems to have a number of possible grounds. One is the notion that terrorism in pursuit of a political objective is never right, or is never right in a democracy, and hence that the claim that it is right in particular circumstances is unacceptable. But even if terrorism never is right – and this would need to be questioned – it does not, of course, follow that the opinion that it sometimes is should be suppressed, for otherwise the mere falsity of an opinion would be a reason for its suppression, and this flies in the face of any belief in freedom of opinion and expression. Nor would it follow that if terrorism itself should be suppressed then opinions of support for it should be also. There may be many reasons against this, not least that it might exacerbate the unrest which gives rise to terrorism. And even if such opinions tend to foster further terrorism, which is doubtful, they cannot, so far, be construed as a threat of or incitement to violence, and hence something to be prevented in the course of preventing terrorism. For political support consists in the judgement that certain acts are right; it need not involve any behaviour intended to promote them (though this is a matter to which we shall return).

A further type of ground for the view that support for terrorism is not admissible to political debate is that it infringes the rules of debate by advocating violence rather than debate in the solution of political problems. The implied games-playing analogy would explain the inadmissibility of an *argumentum ad baculum* in philosophical debate, for example. Threatening to punch one's fellow symposiasts unless they express agreement is no longer conducting a philosophical discussion. The case is quite otherwise in politics. Threats or implied threats of force, or other sanctions affecting the well-being of the disputants, are always a part of the currency of political debate. Indeed it is unclear that we would recognise it as *political* debate – as having to do with *power* – unless they were. Perhaps threats of *violence* fall into a different category from these: they threaten, perhaps, the peace and order on the assumption of which political debate takes place. But, evidently, not all political debate does take place against a background of peace and order. And in any case, as we have just seen, those who enter the debate supporting acts of violence need not be threatening it: they may enter the debate seeking a peaceful, negotiated end to it. In its general form this argument to the illegitimacy of support for terrorism has little merit.

Yet this type of argument tends to be cast in a more specific mode. Political debate in a *democracy*, it is said, rests on the assumption that the contending parties will leave it to the voter to decide the issue. Support for terrorism indicates a disinclination to accept this assumption. Therefore, it is concluded, expressions of such support are not a legitimate part of political debate in a democracy. Unfortunately for this argument, however, the debate in which terrorists seek to enter is characteristically not one on which voters – in their ordinary role as people choosing between the contenders for power within an established democratic State – are *able* to adjudicate. Most terrorist campaigns are waged in support of movements of national secession or reunification and thus challenge State boundaries. The reason for their violent character is that the question of who *should* constitute a State – what body of people has a common political interest on which they can vote democratically – is a question that democratic voting cannot decide and which must therefore be solved by other – and sometimes violent – means. As Ivor Jennings famously expressed it: 'On the surface it seemed reasonable: let the people decide. It was in fact ridiculous because the people cannot decide until somebody decides who the people are.'[6] The assumption of a democratic means for resolving political disputes, on which the argument for restricting the expression of support for violence rests, is simply inapplicable to the kind of case in which such support is most commonly encountered.

It follows that support for terrorism cannot usually be regarded as illegitimate on the grounds that it undercuts an assumption of democratic debate, since democratic debate is commonly inadequate to resolving the issues with which supporters of terrorism are concerned. In these circumstances the question of whether expressions of support for terrorism should be curtailed turns on the extent to which the State should be prepared to countenance political activity designed to upset its constitution or its territorial integrity. Leaving aside for the moment the aspects of this matter which concern the duty of the State to preserve law and order, the view one takes of the permissible extent of legitimate anti-State activity depends on one's conception of the State's relation to its members. Here we can distinguish two contrasting models: one model takes the appropriateness of a certain State in relation to its population as derived from facts about those people independent of their current wishes, tacit or overt, to constitute a single political community (or *nation* in the simplest case). The other takes it to depend on such wishes alone.

The former – involuntarist – model might ground the State's claim to administer the government of a territory on facts about its population's common culture, history, economy or whatever. Such facts are evidently independent of the population's current wish for political unity or otherwise. The pursuit of wishes contrary to the existing State structure can only be viewed as rebellious by a State grounded on such facts. It therefore has no reason to permit their expression, let alone the expression of support for action in pursuit of them. It is on this model that thinking of certain political activities as seditious, and for *that* reason criminal, appears to depend.

Of course, it could be said, dissenting groups may share the involuntarist model and simply differ in their opinions as to what the facts are which should constitute a people as a political community within a State. Certainly this is so. But it provides no obvious reason why the State should allow freedom of expression for anti-State sentiments. Perhaps, on liberal principles, no one's opinion should count for more than anyone else's and so each should get an airing. Yet in the absence of clear principles for resolving this issue continual debate is likely to degenerate into a mutually frustrating and socially destabilising exchange of slogans. Indeed dissentient groups who share the involuntarist model but differ as to the application of it may feel little inclination but to engage in rebellion since they will believe their scope for persuasion to be seriously hampered by the propaganda of the existing State. For its part the existing State may have little choice but to impose its view by force. Restricting the expression of alternatives is a mild form of this.

The other – voluntarist – model is that which underpins modern western notions of popular sovereignty. What constitutes a single political community is the wish of its members to live together as one, and the appropriateness of a given State depends upon its correspondence to such a community. On this model the existence of a single political community – a nation – is, as Renan put it, 'a daily plebiscite'.[7] Evidently, then, the people's wishes as to their appropriate State structure must be permitted free expression. To restrict it is to risk losing the basis in the popular will which grounds the State's claim to administer government. On this model citizens have the right to hear and express views other than those which presuppose a common conception of the national interest and which differ simply on how to realise it. It is not just as voters within an established national framework that their political wishes count, but as voters, actually or figuratively, in a plebiscite eliciting their continued acceptance of it.

On this voluntarist model it is hard to see how activity to change the existing State structures could be regarded as criminal *because* seditious. The notion of sedition has no clear place in it. But it might be argued that on this model such activity must be peaceful, and that expressions of support for violent change can therefore reasonably be proscribed. It might, if actual State structures worked smoothly in accordance with the model, readily adapting to changes in the popular will. Evidently they do not, and, arguably, in principle they cannot. Yet when State structures are not coincident with the wishes of a significant part of the population, and there is no sign of a preparedness to change on the part of the State, it is likely that there will be support for violent opposition. In these circumstances it is natural to expect the State to restrict the expression of this support, although it is hard to see what political justification it could have for doing so. It is no good to argue that certain kinds of constitutional change are available if they are available only on the State's own terms, that is to say, for example, on its own definition of the territories within which plebiscites for secession might be conducted. This is precisely the sort of matter that will be at issue between separatists and the existing State (for example, with respect to the North of Ireland). Indeed, perhaps there is in principle no way of resolving such an issue rationally: why should one side's view of what is a *potentially* separate political community be preferable to the other side's? Yet so long as there is no obvious and readily available way of translating popular wishes into changed State structures there is no good argument to the conclusion that support for terrorism aimed at changing them is not a 'legitimate' political opinion.

POLITICAL SUPPRESSION

Restrictions upon the expression of support for terrorism constitute a form of political suppression (using this term in a way that does not prejudge its justifiability). They exclude certain groups from participation in the political debate that characterises the political life of the community. In the case of the Broadcasting Ban it does this not by censoring the actual views they hold – these views can be reported and discussed. Nor does it make the expression of these views itself punishable – their expression is permissible but not its transmission by the broadcasting media which are crucial to popular political debate. Rather the suppression of people's *voices* detaches and abstracts the views they hold from their lives and actions as individuals participating in a common life and able to enter a dialogue with others. As holders of such views they are excluded from it – they are placed beyond the pale. How are we to interpret this form of political suppression?

The contrast we have drawn between involuntarist and voluntarist models of the State's relation to its members proves helpful in looking at different kinds of political suppression. Broadly speaking, we can regard political suppression aimed at removing or rendering ineffective groups who constitute actual or potential obstacles to political unity as presupposing the involuntarist model. It is because they do not satisfy the qualifying conditions for State membership under the model – through having a distinct culture, history, economic organisation or whatever – that they are treated as obstacles to be removed. The extreme example of such a policy is, of course, genocide. Under the voluntarist model, by contrast, political suppression has a different purpose: it aims at affecting the wishes of the people, including changing the minds of the dissentients, so that there is a coming together of wills to form a single political community, even if the State is not antecedently coincident with any community united by a common political will. Where suppression aims at changing minds voluntarism is presupposed. Political re-education or brainwashing is the paradigm of such suppressive activity, and constitutes the extreme limit of policies of censorship and thought control.

How, in the light of this distinction, might we regard the Broadcasting Ban on the supporters of Northern Irish terrorism? Although ostensibly even-handed it is principally aimed at militant Irish Nationalists. It is therefore possible to regard it as a measure which excludes them from the full range of political activity because their constant reiteration of their Irish nationhood constitutes an obstacle to the integration of the Six Counties into the United Kingdom. Their exclusion represents an admission of their non-membership, rather than a penalty for not acknowledging their membership. The expression of their national distinctness provides the people of Great Britain with reasons to doubt the presupposition that the Six Counties have more in common in terms of culture, history and so forth with Britain than with the rest of Ireland. Its suppression, however, may act as much to confirm this suspicion as to prevent it.

While this may be one element in a confused policy, for the models I have identified are seldom or never found in their pure state in actual political situations, it does not appear to be the principal one.[8] The main aim of the ban is rather to affect people's wishes as to the political community they want to be members of. In part this is to be accomplished simply by the suppression of dissentient voices, thus preserving an *appearance* of a common will, even when one is lacking, precisely in order to *create* it. Surprisingly, I suggest, it also works to change the minds of the dissentient group itself. It does this partly by demoralisation, by sapping their sense of a collective oppositional will by denying it free expression. More interestingly it does so through demonstrating the adverse effects of *non*-membership of the political community. Dissentients are denied a voice in the political debates to which members are admitted. They are taken to have excluded *themselves* from the community by declining to exhibit the will to be part of it, as a result of their activity to make themselves part of another. This is seen as justifying the deprivation of some of the rights of membership, which serves as a warning of the consequences of hopeless opposition.

Yet, on the voluntarist model implied here, political suppression aimed at eliciting a wish to be part of a political community cannot be viewed as *punishment* for dissent. Under this model the wills whose coming together constitutes the community are ostensibly free and unconstrained. The political community could not both be constituted by a common will and legitimise the State if the State *required* the coming together of its subjects' wills. Rather the community would be constituted by subordination to a State which was legitimised otherwise. But if recognition of the State is not required of its subjects then action to induce them to give it by depriving them of the opportunity to participate fully in the political life of the putative community can only seem to them unjust. Seen as such it may well have a tendency to provoke further or greater violence among those who are not cowed by it. Their exclusion from 'legitimate' political activity will lead them to reject those peaceable activities which might be construed as involving recognition of the State.

By refusing to recognise the State, terrorists deny the State's official description of their acts of violence as *criminal*. They insist instead that they are acts of war. The State for its part has no choice but to back up its claim to administer government in its territory by treating acts of violence within it as criminal. For the State to react otherwise is for it to concede the existence of a group internal to its territory who are to be treated like an external aggressor. On either the voluntarist or involuntarist models this would undermine the justification of the State, which resides in its alleged coincidence with a single political community throughout its territory. The most effective way for secessionists to subvert the existing State, then, is to force it into a military posture, and this is the aim of terrorism (although, of course, terrorists, out of weakness, may *rely* on the State adopting only a qualified military response to them). The State, however, will resist such provocation as long as it can, and will deal with terrorism, as it would with any acts of violence, as a breach of the law to be punished or prevented by the civil power, employing troops only to assist the police.

On the voluntarist model there is, as we have seen, a serious tension between excluding a section of the population as not properly part of the predominant political community and adopting this criminalising approach towards its dissentient activities. If this dissentient group actually *is* a distinct political entity then it is, in effect, a subject people to be kept in order by brute force, not through its recognition of the need to obey the law. It is not surprising, therefore, that the reasons offered for excluding a dissentient group from some part of the community's political activity are likely to be that it uses this activity itself in a *criminal* way. It is the *manner*, not the fact, of active dissent that is held to exclude them from political life.

An aspect of the criminalising approach appears in a further reason offered for the Broadcasting Ban, namely that it helps to prevent the *intimidation* of ordinary citizens by terrorist threats. Certainly there is a political purpose here: intimidation might lead to calls for a negotiated settlement or for a full-scale military response, either of which would be unwelcome to the British State. But the principal motive for cutting off opportunities for intimidation is to prevent a criminal act: the offering of threats of murder or bodily harm. It is not as a political act – a warning of the use of force to achieve political objectives – but as a *private* act of individuals conspiring to use violence against their fellow citizens that it is labelled as intimidation and thus as a criminal act to be prevented.

There is no space here to investigate the dual aspect of terrorism itself as both war and crime.[9] But a consequence of its criminal aspect which needs to be emphasised is its resultant character as consisting exclusively of the *private* acts of individuals. The proscription of certain organisations – especially terrorist ones – serves to define the permitted space for *public* speech and action. Beyond it the State recognises only private opinions and private motives. Thus the attempt by terrorist supporters to present their group's actions as political acts (as acts of war, for example, would be) is something that the State seeks to frustrate in denying them full access to the public media. And it denies them access through categorising these actions as merely private – more specifically as criminal – and hence not acts to be admitted to the sphere of public action.

The exclusion of terrorist supporters from the broadcasting media thus relies on an implicit distinction between its availability to public actors and to private agents.[10] To public actors unfettered freedom of expression is permitted because their opinions and objectives are allowed to be relevant to the State's business as it enters political debate in the community. To private agents freedom of expression is restricted when it threatens public order – the state of conformity to laws which preserve civil peace (and perhaps to a broadly shared morality) that is a precondition of a political community. The distinction is itself crucial to defences of freedom of expression (for example, that provided by the Argument from Democracy), since few would wish to argue for totally unfettered freedom, and yet most would wish to argue that some matters might properly be ventilated in the public domain that should not be in the private. One has only to think of the distinction between the scope of personal attacks or personal disclosures in the case of public and of private figures. For our purposes the distinction between threats to bomb an enemy and threats to kill individuals at home or abroad is more relevant. IRA 'warnings' are officially construed as falling into the latter class.

The prevention of *offence* falls into the category of a restriction upon private speech, since it is as private agents that people display the contempt towards others to which offence is taken. A disorderly reaction to contempt is allowed to be natural and comprehensible. As public actors people's attitudes are regarded as judgements upon others whose justification may be questioned, but to which a disorderly reaction is thought unreasonable. In the light of this distinction a further reason for the Broadcasting Ban can be explained. The defence of terrorism, it was said, gave *offence* to those affected by it. Restricting its dissemination for this reason is – like treating it as intimidation – to place it in the realm of private speech which threatens public order. It is not the feelings of those affected but the reactions to which they might give rise that must be the concern of government in imposing this restriction (though, on this score, it may well appear to be unnecessary).

The point that requires emphasis is this: the distinction between the public and the private, of which that between the allowably political and the criminal is an instance, is a distinction imposed by the State. It follows that those who challenge the claims of a given State to administer the government of a territory will take issue with any categorisation of their acts and speech as merely private. They will dispute the established State's way of drawing the distinction and insist upon another which reflects their own aspirations to separate Statehood. The drawing of the distinction is thus itself a controversial political matter. It is not one on which any disinterested philosophical conclusions are possible.

NOTES

1 As the then British Prime Minister, Margaret Thatcher, dubbed it in defending the Broadcasting Ban.
2 Article 19 and Article 10 respectively.
3 See 'Freedom of Expression and Information in the United Kingdom', Article 19, 1991, p.12.
4 *Guardian*, 8 February 1991.
5 Due to A. Meiklejohn, *Political Freedom* (New York, Harper, 1960), pp. 8–28.
6 Quoted by S. French and A. Gutman, 'The Principle of National Self-determination', in V. Held, S. Morgenbesser and Thomas Nagel (eds), *Philosophy, Morality and International Affairs* (New York, Oxford University Press, 1974, pp. 138–53), p. 138.
7 Quoted by S. Benn, 'Nationalism', in P. Edwards (ed.), *Encyclopaedia of Philosophy* (New York, Macmillan, 1967), vol. 5, p. 443.
8 If it were it could not explain the very similar laws on live interviews with terrorists in the Republic of Ireland. These terrorist groups refuse to acknowledge the constitutionality of the existing state – shorn of the Six Counties – just as nationalist groups deny that of Northern Ireland.
9 See Paul Gilbert, 'Terrorism: war or crime?', *Cogito*, 3 (1989), pp. 51–7.
10 See Frank A. Morrow, 'Speech, Expression and the Constitution', in A. Serafini (ed.), *Ethics and Social Concern* (New York, Paragon House, 1989), pp. 528–9.

Chapter 11

Something more important than truth: ethical issues in war reporting

Kevin Williams

Dunkirk represented an appalling defeat for Britain. Large quantities of material were left behind on the beaches. The morale of the British Army was shattered. Men returning home were throwing away their weapons along the railway lines into London. A German invasion was imminent. Tom Hopkinson, then editor of the *Picture Post*, after an appeal from Anthony Eden, decided not to tell the British public the truth about Dunkirk. He, along with his colleagues in Fleet Street, believed the truth would demoralise people and make them less able to resist an invasion. Instead the press presented Dunkirk as some sort of triumph and attempted to keep Britain in good heart. Hopkinson, rather than tell just how bad things were, filled the *Picture Post* with articles full of practical ideas for resisting an invasion.

> I believed that if we all resisted for a year, the Americans would be bound to come into the war, and would beat the Germans. It was the truth of the imagination, not the truth of external reality.[1]

Hopkinson's decision flew in the face of the military truth of the situation – it was for him a 'spiritual truth'. He believed that 'in wartime there is sometimes something more important than truth'.

This chapter asks whether it is the proper task of the journalist in wartime to be more concerned with the 'truth of the imagination' than with the 'truth of external reality', the latter after all being the basic raw material of journalism. In wartime journalism is faced with a number of ethical problems. Should graphic pictures of the dead be shown? Should the grief of families who have lost loved ones on the battlefield be intruded on? Should correspondents report from the enemy's side? Should reporters accede to restrictions placed by the military on their movements in the war zone? These are all important concerns in the reporting of war. But at their heart is a basic ethical dilemma about the role of the journalist at times of armed conflict involving his or her country. How should war correspondents resolve the competing claims made by their work and by their country?

We will examine how this clash of allegiances has been resolved in different armed conflicts. The arguments of those who seek to uphold the basic tenet of journalism, to report events in an objective and detached manner, will be discussed. These will be compared with the views of those who believe journalists in wartime have to accept their obligations as citizens of the country they live in. It will be argued that this clash of allegiances is usually resolved in favour of the journalist's obligations as a citizen. However, journalism works with a narrow interpretation of citizenship which ties it closely to official views and explanations of events. This is a response to the routines and practices of journalism rather than any conspiracy between journalism and the State. War exposes most starkly the gap between the rhetoric and reality that exists at the heart of the profession of journalism.

TELLING THE TRUTH

It was John Delane, the editor of *The Times*, who laid down the standard by which war correspondents should report. In response to an enquiry from his man in the field, William Howard Russell, the 'first and greatest' of war reporters, as to whether he (Russell) should record the suffering and misery he saw about him in the Crimea, Delane said: 'Continue as you have done, to tell the truth and as much of it as you can, and leave such comment as may be dangerous to us, who are out of danger.'[2] Russell continued to report what he saw and the result was that his reporting brought down a government. Delane's word and Russell's action set the standard to which subsequent correspondents have aspired. One such was Tom Hopkinson himself. During the Korean War he took a view about the media's responsibility entirely different from the one he held in the Second World War. When reporter James Cameron and photographer Bert Hardy sent back an account of the brutality with which Britain's ally South Korea treated its prisoners of war, the *Picture Post*'s owner, Edward Hulton, said the article would 'give aid and comfort to the enemy' and told Hopkinson to spike it. Hopkinson refused and Hulton sacked him. For Hopkinson this was a situation where the truth, however unpalatable and bad for morale, had to be told. On this occasion nothing was more important than truth.

The distinction Hopkinson would perhaps draw between the situations concerns the nature of the two wars. The Second World War was a matter of national survival. There was a direct threat to Britain's way of life. Defeat would have resulted in subjugation. The Korean War, on the other hand, at least as far as the British public was concerned, was in essence a police action happening on the other side of the world. There was no national emergency. There was no direct threat to national life. It is only when the very survival of a society is threatened that the truth can be interfered with.

However, the distinction between these two kinds of conflict has become blurred in the post-war period. Since 1945 most of the wars in which Britain has been involved have been like the Korean War – undeclared, far off and no threat. Those seeking to stress the war correspondent's patriotic duty have used the experience of the Second World War to recast these modern conflicts as wars of national survival. Whether it is casting Galtieri or Saddam Hussein in the role of Hitler or evoking the spirit of 'our finest hour', the Second World War is used to justify the demand that journalism should be subservient to the needs of the war effort. While Hopkinson may feel he was justified in suppressing the truth about Dunkirk his words and actions have set a precedent which others less interested in telling the truth in wartime have used to deny the public knowledge about what is going on.

WINNING THE WAR

What is thought by many to be more important than telling the truth about war is *winning* it. One family at war has put this viewpoint very clearly. During the Falklands conflict – an undeclared war more than half a world away – Max Hastings quoted the words of his father, a celebrated World War Two reporter: 'When one's nation is at war, reporting becomes an extension of the war effort. Objectivity only comes back into fashion when the black-out comes down.'[3] Hastings gave a clear exposition of his philosophy of the role of journalism at war on his return home from the South Atlantic. He wrote:

> I felt my function was simply to identify totally with the interests and feelings of that force [the Task Force] . . . when one was

> writing one's copy one thought: beyond telling everybody what the men around me were doing, what can one say that is likely to be most helpful in winning this war.[4]

For the military this is how the war correspondent should behave – as one US general said during the Vietnam War, the press should be 'on team'. But what does being 'on team' mean? It is accepted that operational security and the protection of the lives of servicemen and women should govern what correspondents can and cannot say. But winning a war involves more than preserving operational security. Other things are deemed necessary and desirable by the authorities: the maintenance of morale at home and at the front, ensuring commitment to the cause, and making certain that the 'enemy' is throughly hated. These are all part of the propaganda efforts of the State. The media can play and have played a role in all these activities. This raises the question of the extent to which journalists should compromise their profession in the service of 'winning the war'.

Winning the war, especially when the national community is not threatened, will always be more important to some sections of society than others. If it is an imperialist venture, only some people have to gain from territorial acquisition. If it is a neo-colonial enterprise motivated by global strategic considerations it may not exercise the average citizen. Therefore wars and the object of winning them in such situations will have to be 'sold' to the public. This often involves the manipulation of the truth in order to maintain popular support for war.

THE PUBLIC'S RIGHT TO KNOW

Ultimately whichever role the war correspondent chooses to guide his or her reporting it has to be legitimated in a democratic society by an appeal to the public interest. The public's right to know is the guiding principle for honest and open reporting in war or peace. As one American newspaper editor clearly put it during the Second World War: 'The final decision rests with the people. And the people, so that they may make up their minds, must be given the facts, even in war time, or, perhaps, especially in war time.'[5]

But what if the public do not want to know? Peregrine Worsthorne argues that the public are not interested in knowing the truth if it jeopardises the war effort: 'Public opinion, if I am not mistaken, takes the view that in time of war the authorities should be left to get on with the job of winning without having to satisfy media curiousity at every turn.'[6] Worsthorne's point received support from the polls taken of US and British public opinion during the Gulf War. Nearly 8 out of 10 Americans supported the Pentagon's restrictions on journalists covering the war while 6 out of 10 said they believed there should be 'more control'.[7] This caused a great deal of anxiety for journalists. The letters editor of *The Independent*, after reviewing the contents of his post bag on the war, found that: 'the urge to censor in wartime is not restricted to authorities, and our claim that we wish to print the truth as we find it, on behalf of our readers, is perhaps a little thinner than we might like to contemplate'.[8]

This point about the public and their desire to know is very important in any discussion of the reporting of truth in war and it is something to which we will return. But to examine Hopkinson's proposition in more detail it is necessary to look at the barriers to telling the truth in wartime.

CENSORSHIP

There are many obstacles to the truth being told in wartime, although it should be stressed that these also apply in peacetime but are less apparent. War should not be seen as a special case of how the media works. War highlights and intensifies many of the things that happen in peacetime. As Robert Harris said of the Falklands War: 'It briefly illuminated aspects of British society usually hidden from view. It exposed habitual abuses by the armed forces, Government, Whitehall and the media; it did not create them.'[9] Censorship is one such abuse.

In democratic societies the only area in which it is openly accepted that censorship has a part to play is in the field of military security. The Ministry of Defence has said that the essence of good warfare is secrecy. Military commanders have been worried by newspaper reports jeopardising military operations and putting servicemen's and women's lives at risk since the beginning of the last century. The Duke of Wellington complained to the Prime Minister, Lord Liverpool, about the problem during the Peninsular Wars.[10] However the application of censorship has not simply concerned itself with the prevention of operational information reaching the enemy. The history of censorship in wartime indicates that it has been used to 'sell' wars to the public and maintain and enhance morale at home by dishonest means. Censorship has been used to hide military incompetence and inefficiency resulting in the loss of servicepeople's lives. Heavy casualties and atrocities perpetuated by 'our' side have been covered up. Accounts considered in bad taste or too harrowing have fallen victim to the censor's blue pencil. Rivalries between different branches of the armed forces have also resulted in the suppressing of material.

The Falklands conflict saw material censored on the grounds of taste: army and navy officers would preview all film used by the BBC and tell them, among other things, not to use a picture of a body in a bag, not to use the phrase 'horribly burned' and not to show an interview with a Harrier pilot who admitted he had been 'scared fartless' on one mission.[11] The Ministry of Defence referred to this process as 'clearance' – during the Gulf War it was called 'guidance' – rather than 'censorship'. This perhaps was a sensible precaution given the absence of any legal basis for censorship in either conflict as there was no formal declaration of war. It also reflects the fact that censorship is an emotive term in a country which calls itself a democracy. Sometimes any reference to its existence has to be concealed to avoid public outcry as during the Falklands War when the word 'censored' was censored from journalists' reports. But whatever censorship is called, the effect is the same: to sanitise war and minimise, in the public's eyes, the human cost.

The use of censorship to help sanitise war reached new heights during the Gulf conflict. For Philip Knightley the war marked an alarming development in the history of censorship. There was an additional aim: 'to alter public perception of the nature of war itself, particularly the fact that civilians die in war'.[12] The picture that the authorities painted was of a war without death. The military served up video images of 'smart' bombs taking out buildings with pinpoint accuracy while 'minimising' casualties. Military briefers told of the 'surgical nature' of air strikes. There were few pictures of bodies during the period of the fighting. Language was used to hide the killing – for 'collateral damage' read 'dead civilians', for 'degradation of enemy capacity' read 'dead soldiers', for 'soft targets' read 'people' and for 'laying down a carpet' read 'saturation bombing'. The reluctance of military briefers to discuss casualties further added to the idea that this was a war which did not involve actual people.[13]

The rationale for this policy was that the public will no longer support any war involving a large number of civilian casualties. This is the 'lesson' military and civilian leaders in the West have learned from Vietnam which has become the paradigm for understanding the role of media in contemporary conflicts. The media, especially the electronic media, are believed to have 'lost' the war by showing the public at home the true realities of the battlefield. There is little evidence to support this view.[14] The images served up by television in the formative years of the fighting were not as graphic and as bloody as imagined and poll data actually indicated that TV coverage did not make the American public less supportive. For example, a poll conducted for *Newsweek* in 1967 found that 64 per cent of those asked said that TV coverage had made them more supportive.[15]

For others the reasons for censorship are more straightforward. One local newspaper accepted the 'severe but understandable restrictions' on the reporting of the Gulf War because the 'realities of battle, especially the inevitable casualties, can seriously upset ordinary people'.[16] So-called ordinary people according to one survey appear to support the newspaper's viewpoint. The survey found, for example, that only 8 per cent of those questioned thought it acceptable to show close-up pictures of British dead.[17] Those who agreed that such pictures should not be shown did not however give as their reason that they would be upset by them. As 36 per cent of them stated: 'we have enough imagination to work it out for ourselves'. Rather they were concerned for the relatives of those killed.

The incident during the Gulf War that brought to the surface these concerns about the impact of the horrors of war was the death of 400 civilians in the Al-Ameriya bunker in Baghdad. Reporting of this tragedy, especially the TV coverage, was criticised. A Ministry of Defence spokesperson said that 'the general public did not want to see these things'.[18] For the *Daily Telegraph*, showing pictures of the bombing just gave comfort to the enemy; it inadvertently addressed the 'agenda of Saddam'.[19] The aim presumably was to exploit public sensibilities by placing injury to civilians on western TV screens – or as the *Telegraph* put it 'bad presentation could weaken morale'. While it could be said that television can make it more difficult to prosecute war if it humanises the cannon-fodder, the arguments used against showing pictures such as those of the Al-Ameriya bombing underestimate the resilience of the public. As Charles Mohr has pointed out: 'most wars literally, not merely photographically, go through people's living rooms' without a consequent collapse of the will to fight.[20] It is also worth noting that TV could make war 'less real' to its audience. Michael Arlen, who is credited with coining the term the 'living room war' in relation to Vietnam, argues that war is 'diminished in part by the physical size of the television screen'; despite all industry's advances it can show only 'a picture of men three inches tall shooting other men three inches tall'.[21]

But whatever the impact, does the audience have a right to be protected from such images? Wars prosecuted by democratic societies are done so in the name of the people. If the public supports a war then it has a responsibility for all the consequences. Citizens have rights and responsibilities and surely one of the responsibilities in wartime is to see – or at least be provided with the opportunity to see – the price being paid to prosecute the war, whether this is the body of your neighbour's son or innocent civilians killed in the crossfire. Even if people do not want to accept their responsibilties it is difficult to argue that they have a right to be protected from seeing what happens on the battlefield. This would appear to deny a necessary democratic impulse.

SELF-CENSORSHIP

Censorship goes hand in hand with self-censorship by journalists. Journalists at war have censored themselves for a number of reasons: because they expect to be censored, because they or their editors decide that it is not in the 'national interest' to publish, because of their commitment to a cause or simply because of personal loyalty to the soldiers they accompany. Most journalists paradoxically appear to be more comfortable with some form of censorship in wartime. The Vietnam War was an open war, fought without formal censorship. Lack of censorship led to more self-censorship among correspondents. With little or no guidance reporters on occasions were uncertain of what to write for fear of endangering life or giving away vital military information. Uncomfortable with taking the responsibility for what they wrote, they sought to shift the onus back onto the military authorities. Several Saigon bureau chiefs appealed for the introduction of field censorship.[22]

Notions of 'patriotism' can get in the way of telling the truth in wartime. Most news organisations are national organisations. ITN saw itself during the Falklands War not simply as the purveyor of information about what was going on in the South Atlantic but also as the guardian of national morale and the national interest. ITN took this role so seriously that in its submission to the House of

Commons Select Committee inquiry into the handling of information during the war it opposed the restrictions placed on reports coming back from the battlefront on these grounds: 'Great opportunities were missed for the positive projection of the single minded energy and determination of the British people in their support of the task force.'[23]

The BBC appeared to have had difficulty in reconciling its reporting role with that of its duty as a national organisation. Certain programmes were criticised for treating Argentine and British claims with the same weight. A *Panorama* programme which examined domestic opposition to the war as well as presenting the Argentine case was described as an 'odious and subversive travesty' which 'dishonoured the right to freedom of speech in this country'.[24] The skirmishes between the BBC and the Government were seen to reinforce the view that 'in times of war a conflict of interests inevitably exists between the government and the BBC'.[25] However the patriotic partiality of the BBC is clearly indicated by the minutes of its News and Current Affairs Committee (NCA). This Committee which comprises senior BBC management and programme makers met regularly throughout the war to discuss the reporting. The Committee made a clear statement about its view of the BBC's coverage in a meeting on the day after the *Panorama* controversy: 'the weight of BBC coverage has been concerned with government statements and policy'.[26] Fear was expressed in another meeting about reports which would 'undermine the national will'.[27] The BBC felt it was unjustly accused and had taken its duty as the *British* Broadcasting Corporation seriously. According to one MP the fault lay in the 'inability of [BBC] management to supervise producers properly'.[28]

Tensions between the editorial office and the reporter in the field are common in wartime. During the Vietnam War many correspondents complained about the problem of getting editors to accept their versions of events. One *Time* reporter in Vietnam states that 'many editors ignored what their correspondents were telling them in favour of the Washington version' put out by the Pentagon.[29] British editors have also had great trouble in believing what their man or woman at the front tells them. It is difficult to forget the on-screen interrogation of the BBC man in Baghdad by his colleagues in London following his report of the death of civilians in the Al-Ameriya bunker. The BBC, while they make much in retrospect of Richard Dimbleby's emotionally charged reporting from Belsen, did not initially broadcast his report because they did not believe him. It was only used after others confirmed his report.[30] It is not only the correspondent's conception of his or her patriotic duty but also the view of the media organisation he or she works for that shapes the telling of the truth in wartime.

The motivation behind journalists concealing or not telling the truth is not necessarily simply straightforward patriotism. It can also be the product of political commitment of a more general kind to one side or another. The Spanish Civil War is a case in point. Many journalists who covered the war 'took sides'. On the Republican side some reporters were also fighting in the International Brigades which strengthened their own personal commitment to the cause – Hemingway, Orwell and Claude Cockburn among them. Herbert Matthews of the *New York Times* spoke for these reporters when he said: 'I would always opt for open, honest bias. A newspaperman should work with his heart as well as his mind.'[31] Knightley documents one incident during the war when a journalist, Louis Fischer, who worked for the *New Statesman* and whose reports were read in newspapers throughout the world, filed a dispatch which reported that the Republican militia were demoralised. Cockburn and a Soviet reporter were furious, arguing that this dispatch had done more to undermine the Republican cause than 'thirty British MPs working for Franco' – though both accepted that Fischer's reports were true. Fischer responded by saying his readers had a right to read the truth but Cockburn rejected this:

> Who gave [the readers] such a right? Perhaps when they have exerted themselves enough to alter the policy of their bloody government and the Fascists are beaten in Spain, they will have such a right. This isn't an abstract question. It's a shocking war.[32]

Cockburn presents us with a novel proposition: that being told the facts about what is happening in a war is something that has to be earned by the public, by demonstrating its support for the right side. At one level this will not do – it gives the journalist the power to decide who has the right to know and who does not. It also rests on an assumption that war reporting should be a part of the propaganda effort. Cockburn is perhaps more honest than many of his fellow correspondents because that is very often what war reporting is: in all the wars cited in this chapter journalism has been (ab)used in this way. Even if the Republic's cause was just that is no reason for suppressing part of the truth about what was going on. Knightley concludes:

> There can be no validity in Cockburn's attitude. If readers have no right to facts, but only to what a war correspondent feels it is in his side's best interest to reveal, then there is no use for war correspondents at all.[33]

This statement assumes a slightly idealistic view of readers, as rational actors who weigh up the information they receive and then make up their mind as to the truth of what they are told. Often readers – or viewers – are seeking to have their prejudices confirmed. This explains why they consume certain media products as opposed to others. The *Daily Worker*'s version of the truth of the Spanish Civil War differed from that of the *Daily Express*. However, the reporting of Cockburn and his colleagues in Spain did a disservice to their own side. Their reports about the conduct of the war led to over-optimism about the chances of a Republican victory and ignored the problems their side faced.

Commitment can be for personal as well as ideological reasons. Reporters at the front can build up a strong empathy with the soldiers they live alongside. They develop a strong sense of obligation which is the result of their dependence on the soldiers for food, shelter and most importantly, safety. John Shirley, who reported the Falklands War for *The Sunday Times*, admitted to having a 'love affair with the military' while with the Task Force. He did not report seeing bodies in a 'terrible state' because he did not think it was 'fair' – he had, on his own admission, become too close emotionally to some of the soldiers.[34] Limitations of the truth of war then arise out of the comradeship and the necessary intimacy between war correspondents and those with whom they share the sharp end of battle.

The military use such emotional bonds for their own purpose. In the Gulf, in the cause of enhancing reporters' access to the battlefield, the authorities set up arrangements which allowed them to dictate the terms of trade. The pool system was based on the calculation that by placing reporters alongside troops a sense of identification and empathy would develop. Such was the bonding of journalists to their units that some began writing like soldiers: 'I think I can say, on behalf of the whole 4th Armoured Brigade . . .'.[35] In return for being placed with frontline troops pool reporters accepted restrictions on what they could say and where they could go. Any infringement of the rules could result in a reporter being excluded from the battlefield.

Within the mainstream media differences emerged between the

pool reporters and those who attempted to report the war independently, the so-called 'unilateralists'. Without the refusal of some reporters to participate in the pool system and their attempts to see for themselves what was happening many aspects of this war would not have reached the public. Unilateral reporting resulted in tension with the military authorities but what is more interesting is the response of pool reporters. Robert Fisk, a unilateralist, relates his account of trying to report the Iraqi capture of Khafji in the early days of the conflict. Pool reporters, he says, were kept 15 miles from Khafji, misled by their military escorts, and filed stories that the town had been recaptured by Allied forces. Fisk travelled to the scene to investigate and found out that long after Prime Minister John Major had announced outside 10 Downing Street that the town had been liberated, fighting was still going on. Fisk's presence in Khafji provoked a bitter response from fellow correspondents. One US TV reporter, a member of the military pool, told him: 'You asshole; you'll prevent us from working. You're not allowed here. Get out, get back to Dahran.' For many reporters 'the privileges of the pool and the military rules attached to it were more important than the right of a journalist to do his job'.[36]

For the war correspondent 'being there' is as important as reporting the truth of events. This need has been accentuated by the advent of television. Eyewitness reports are increasingly seen as the measure of 'good journalism'. Thus it could be said that the 'privileges' of being part of the pool in the Saudi desert were seen as an essential ingredient of 'doing the job'. The way journalists do their job is as significant for the nature of truth in wartime as censorship and self-censorship. It also perhaps raises a question as to whether the claims of a war correspondent's work and the claims of his or her country are as irreconcilable as Tom Hopkinson implies.

DOING THE JOB

Many obstacles to telling the truth in wartime arise from the routines and practices of journalism. For example, journalists work in a competitive environment. There is pressure to be 'first with the news'. Kim Sabido, the Independent Radio News reporter in the Falklands, accused some of his colleagues of outright lying 'perpetrated, I believe, in a blind desire to be first with the news instead of being truthful'.[37] Such competition is increased in wartime. War is a 'big story' in which reporters can establish a reputation quickly and advance their careers.

There is pressure to get the story in on deadline (or to get it in at all). A Reuters reporter covering the civil war in Angola accepted that CIA efforts to plant fabricated stories which were detrimental to Cuban involvement in the war were largely successful because the CIA were able to manipulate him.[38] He said that when filing these stories he did not know whether they were true or not. He pleaded overwork (sixteen hours per day for a couple of months) and his overriding responsibility to keep a steady flow of information to his head office. The reporter had neither the time nor the resources to check the accuracy of all the information coming into his Lusaka office for dissemination worldwide. Contrary to the common perception of journalists as hard-working, rigorous seekers of truth, for many of them, and particularly in the midst of a gruelling and confusing war, truth must take second place to the swift production of copy.

The Reuters man in Lusaka had much of his material reprinted in the British press. One *Daily Telegraph* specialist correspondent, whose paper published the CIA-invented stories received via Reuters, argued that it is not the responsibility of the reporter to determine whether stories are true or not but simply to reproduce them and acknowledge their source. 'I've no idea whether they were true or not, I just report what I am told . . . it is not our job to decide if it is true or not.'[39] News reporting is a balancing act involving what Glasser describes as 'conflicting truth claims'.[40] These are often reported regardless of their validity. Any assessment of the claims is based on notions of their 'news value'. To challenge such claims is to call into question the journalist's objectivity. Dorman observes that 'such a principle overlooks the possibility that one or both claimants are lying, misinformed, fantasizing, or, more likely, slanting their statements towards the particular conclusions they want their audience to reach'.[41] For many news reporters truth is not a matter of reporting what has happened but the accurate reproduction of what someone has told you has happened. This version of the truth fits more comfortably with the working practices of journalism.

WHOSE TRUTH?

The above discussion has indicated the fragile nature of truth in wartime. Censorship, political commitment, patriotic duty, the routines and limitations of daily journalism are just a few obstacles to the public ever getting a truthful account of war, particularly when their own country is involved. It is clear that objectivity and balance are, in the journalist's mind, not necessarily the same as the truth. Perhaps it is a misunderstanding to see journalists as having to wrestle with weighty ethical decisions about what to report; rather the routines and practices of their work have already made those decisions for them.

Hopkinson believes that a sensible line can be drawn between the journalist's responsibility to the truth and responsibility to country. In times of grave peril to the nation the 'truth of external reality' has to take second place to maintaining public morale and ensuring national survival. But who draws this line? Who is to decide what the public should and should not be told? And on what grounds do they decide that a situation is sufficiently threatening to subvert the truth?

For Hopkinson the decision rests in the hands of a 'few responsible people'. It was the Government and its 'insider' friends in the media who decided that the British people should not receive the full and unpleasant facts about Dunkirk. Such a decision undermines the democratic notion of a society as a collectivity founded on an informed debate between equals. It sets the 'governed' apart from the 'government'. It also takes a dim view of the resilience and maturity of the 'governed' – that the public 'out there' are too immature, fragile or stupid to be trusted with the truth at all times.

The Gulf War is used to justify not telling the public the whole truth on the grounds that they do not want to be told. Edwin Godkin, who covered the Crimean War for the *Daily News* said that the presence of correspondents 'brought home to the War Office the fact that the public had something to say about the conduct of wars and that they are not the concern exclusively of sovereigns and statesmen'.[42] This has been the basis of journalism's presence at war ever since. The public's desire not to know or to be told only what it wants to hear is not an argument against recording the truth without restraint. Public ignorance or indifference is no justification for reproduction of the authorised truth. When the flow of information in a democratic society is controlled by the authorities and when military considerations take precedence over all other considerations then democracy itself is threatened.

Even during times of national survival a democracy should maintain awareness of the importance of the truth; otherwise it may win the war but diminish its democracy. Every time journalists make decisions not to tell the truth, as they see it, whether it is on their own initiative or at the behest of the military or government, then it sets a precedent for the future. It further legitimises the idea that the public should not be trusted all the time. It is a short step from this to saying that if the public is likely to disagree with what its government is doing then it should not be trusted with the truth. The Gulf War, with no direct threat to western national security, provided, as the BBC's John Simpson pointed out, the unedifying sight and sound of free men and women clamouring for chains. 'It is depressing, at a time when there is no equivalent state of national emergency, to hear demands that British journalism should subserve the ends of propaganda rather than the civilised principles of openness and honesty.'[43]

Simpson, of course, was comparing the Gulf War with our great war of national survival, the Second World War. Those seeking to be told less rather than more used the reporting of this war as their precedent. They should perhaps have heeded the assessment made by Charles Lynch, a World War Two correspondent, who said of his own, and his colleagues, performance:

> It's humiliating to look back on what we wrote during the war. It was crap . . . . We were a propaganda arm of our governments. At the start the censors enforced that, but by the end we were our own censors. We were cheerleaders. I suppose there wasn't an alternative at the time. It was total war. But, for God's sake, let's not glorify our role. It wasn't good journalism at all.[44]

Hopkinson did not write the truth of Dunkirk but some of his colleagues did write lies. 'Bloody Marvellous' trumpeted a *Daily Mirror* headline. It may be difficult for the war correspondent to tell the truth all the time. But it should be easy to distinguish between not telling the truth and telling lies. It is perhaps an indulgence to see the history of war reporting as tormented correspondents wrestling with their consciences about what they should or should not report. On the whole many correspondents have been indifferent to the official manipulation of truth in wartime. They prefer a quiet life, getting on with doing the job and realising their ambitions. Perhaps telling the truth – not propaganda – sits uncomfortably with the work of the war correspondent.

NOTES

1 Sir Tom Hopkinson's remarks are taken from two sources: a talk he gave to the M.Sc.(Econ.) course in Media Studies at the University of Wales, Cardiff, in August 1986, and an interview he gave for David Jessel's documentary *Trumpets and Typewriters*, which appeared on BBC TV in 1983.
2 Philip Knightley, *The First Casualty: The War Correspondent as Hero, Propagandist and Myth Maker* (London, Quartet, 1982), p. 12.
3 Quoted in Patricia Holland, 'In These Times When Men Walk Tall: The Popular Press and the Falklands Conflict', *Cencrastus* (1984), no. 17, p. 19.
4 Quoted in Robert Harris, *Gotcha: The Media, the Government and the Falklands Conflict* (London, Faber & Faber, 1983), p. 135.
5 Quoted in Knightley, op. cit., p. 253.
6 *UK Press Gazette*, 18 February 1991.
7 *Index on Censorship*, 20 (1991), no. 4/5, p. 34.
8 ibid., p. 7.
9 Harris, op. cit., p. 152.
10 Trevor Royle, *War Report* (London, Grafton, 1989), p. 18.
11 Harris, op. cit., p. 60.
12 Philip Knightley, 'Here is the Patriotically Censored News', *Index on Censorship*, 20 (1991), no. 4/5, pp. 4–5.
13 The estimated casualties in the Gulf War have been put at above 200,000 people. One thing common to most war correspondents is that they have never questioned the institution of war (see Knightley, *The First Casualty*). This has often led to scant attention being paid to the victims of war, the civilians caught in the midst of the fighting. In modern conflicts, especially the Vietnam and Gulf wars, there has been an additional reluctance to face up to the racist nature of these wars (see Knightley, ibid.; and Edward Pearce, 'War Guilt, Zinoviev and the Boring Canadian: The Press and the War', in Victoria Brittain (ed.), *The Gulf Between Us* (London, Virago, 1991), pp. 97–106).
14 See Daniel Hallin, *The Uncensored War: The Media and Vietnam* (New York, Oxford University Press, 1986), and Robert Entman and David Paletz, 'The War in South East Asia: Tunnel Vision on Television', in William C. Adams (ed.), *Television Coverage of International Affairs* (Norwood, NJ, Ablex, 1982).
15 Edward Epstein, *Between Fact and Fiction* (New York, Vintage, 1975).
16 *South Wales Echo*, 11 January 1991.
17 David Morrison, 'Conditional Truths', *Spectrum* (1991), no. 2, p. 11.
18 *UK Press Gazette*, 17 June 1991.
19 Quoted in *Index on Censorship*, 20 (1991), no. 4/5, p. 8.
20 Derrik Mercer, Geoff Mungham and Kevin Williams, *The Fog of War: The Media on the Battlefield* (London, Heinemann, 1987), p. 225.
21 Michael Arlen, *The Living Room War* (New York, Viking, 1968), p. 8.
22 Mercer, Mungham and Williams, op. cit., p. 254.
23 Quoted in Harris, op. cit., p. 106.
24 ibid., p. 80.

25 ibid., p. 91.
26 NCA Minutes, 11 May 1982, quoted in Glasgow University Media Group, *War and Peace News* (Milton Keynes, Open University Press, 1985), p. 17.
27 NCA Minutes, 8 June 1982 quoted in Glasgow University Media Group, ibid., p. 15.
28 Harris, op. cit., p. 82.
29 Knightley, *The First Casualty*, p. 344.
30 ibid., p. 313.
31 Quoted in ibid., p. 177.
32 Quoted in ibid., p. 180.
33 ibid., p. 181.
34 Remarks made in *Trumpets and Typewriters*, BBC TV, 1983.
35 *UK Press Gazette*, 3 June 1991.
36 Robert Fisk, 'Free to Report What We're Told', *The Independent*, 6 February 1991.
37 Quoted in Harris, op. cit., p. 143.
38 'Standard Techniques', *Diverse Reports*, Channel 4 TV, 30 October 1985.
39 ibid.
40 Thomas Glasser, 'Objectivity Precludes Responsibility', in Ray Eldon Hiebert and Carol Reuss (eds), *Impact of Mass Media* (London, Longman, 1985), pp. 51–9.
41 William Dorman, 'Peripheral Vision: US Journalism and the Third World', *World Policy Journal* (Summer 1986), p. 423.
42 Knightley, *The First Casualty* p. 17.
43 John Simpson, 'Free Men Clamouring for Chains', *Index on Censorship*, 20 (1991), no. 4/5, pp. 3–4.
44 Quoted in Knightley, *The First Casualty*, p. 317.
45 This chapter could not have been written without the words, observations and encouragement of Clare Hudson and Geoff Mungham.

Select bibliography on ethics, journalism and the media

Barendt, Eric, *Freedom of Speech*, Oxford, Oxford University Press, 1985.

Bayles, Michael D., *Professional Ethics*, 2nd edn, Belmont, CA, Wadsworth, 1988.

Birkinshaw, Patrick, *Freedom of Information: The Law, the Practice and the Ideal*, London, Weidenfeld & Nicolson, 1988.

Bok, Sissela, *Lying: Moral Choice in Public and Private Life*, London, Quartet, 1980.

——, *Secrets: On the Ethics of Concealment and Revelation*, New York, Oxford University Press, 1984.

Brown, Geoffrey, *The Information Game: Ethical Issues in a Microchip World*, London, Humanities Press, 1990.

Callahan, Joan C. (ed.), *Ethical Issues in Professional Life*, New York, Oxford University Press, 1988.

Christians, Clifford G. and Covert, Catherine L., *Teaching Ethics in Journalism Education*, New York, Hastings Center, 1980.

Christians, Clifford G., Rotzoll, Kim B. and Fackler, Mark, *Media Ethics: Cases and Moral Reasoning*, 3rd edn, New York, Longman, 1991.

Cline, Victor B. (ed.), *Where Do You Draw the Line? An Exploration into Media Violence, Pornography and Censorship*, Provo, UT, Brigham Young University Press, 1974.

Cohen, Phil and Gardner, Carl (eds), *It Ain't Half Racist, Mum: Fighting Racism in the Media*, London, Comedia/Campaign against Racism in the Media, 1982.

Cooper, Thomas W., *Communication Ethics and Global Change*, New York, Longman, 1989.

Curran, James (ed.), *Bending Reality: The State of the Media*, London, Pluto/Campaign for Press and Broadcasting Freedom, 1986.

Curran, James and Gurevitch, Michael (eds), *Mass Media and Society*, London, Edward Arnold, 1991.

Curran, James and Seaton, Jean, *Power without Responsibility: The Press and Broadcasting in Britain*, 4th edn, London, Routledge, 1991.

Day, Louis A., *Ethics in Media Communications: Cases and Controversies*, Belmont, CA, Wadsworth, 1991.

Elliott, Deni (ed.), *Responsible Journalism*, Beverly Hills, CA, Sage, 1986.

Evans, Harold, *Good Times, Bad Times*, London, Weidenfeld & Nicolson, 1983.
Ewing, K.D. and Gearty, C.A., *Freedom under Thatcher: Civil Liberties in Modern Britain*, Oxford, Oxford University Press, 1990.
Fink, Conrad C., *Media Ethics: In the Newsroom and Beyond*, New York, McGraw-Hill, 1988.
Garnham, Nicholas, *Capitalism and Communications: Global Culture and the Economics of Information*, London, Sage, 1990.
Glasgow University Media Group, *Bad News*, London, Routledge, 1976.
—— *More Bad News*, London, Routledge, 1980.
—— *Really Bad News*, London, Routledge, 1981.
—— *War and Peace News*, Milton Keynes, Open University Press, 1985.
Goldman, Alan, *The Moral Foundations of Professional Ethics*, Totowa, NJ, Rowman & Littlefield, 1980.
Goodwin, H. Eugene, *Groping for Ethics in Journalism*, 2nd edn, Ames, IA, Iowa State University Press, 1987.
Harris, Nigel G.E., *Professional Codes of Conduct in the United Kingdom: A Directory*, London, Mansell, 1989.
Harris, Robert, *Gotcha: The Media, the Government and the Falklands Conflict*, London, Faber & Faber, 1983.
Hewitt, Patricia, *Privacy: The Information Gatherers*, London, National Council for Civil Liberties, 1977.
—— *The Abuse of Power: Civil Liberties in the United Kingdom*, Oxford, Martin Robertson, 1982.
Hillyard, Paddy and Percy-Smith, Janie, *The Coercive State*, London, Fontana, 1988.
Hodgson, Godfrey, *Truth, Journalism and the Gulf* (Fifth James Cameron Memorial Lecture), London, City University, 1991.
Hollingsworth, Mark, *The Press and Political Dissent*, London, Pluto, 1985.
Hooper, David, *Official Secrets: The Use and Abuse of the Act*, London, Secker & Warburg, 1987.
Horton, Philip C. (ed.), *The Third World and Press Freedom*, New York, Praeger, 1978.
Hulteng, John L., *Playing it Straight: A Practical Discussion of the Ethical Principles of the American Society of Newspaper Editors*, Chester, CT, American Society of Newspaper Editors, 1981.
—— *The Messenger's Motives: Ethical Problems of the News Media*, 2nd edn, Englewood Cliffs, NJ, Prentice-Hall, 1985.
Jansen, S.C., *Censorship: The Knot that Binds Power and Knowledge*, Oxford, Oxford University Press, 1988.
Johannesen, Richard L., *Ethics in Human Communication*, 3rd edn, Prospect Heights, IL, Waveland Press, 1990.
Jones, J. Clement, *Mass Media Codes of Ethics and Councils: A Comparative International Study on Professional Standards*, Paris, Unesco, 1980.
Jones, Mervyn (ed.), *Privacy*, Newton Abbot, David & Charles, 1974.
Keane, John, *The Media and Democracy*, Oxford, Polity Press, 1991.
Klaidman, Stephen and Beauchamp, Tom L., *The Virtuous Journalist*, New York, Oxford University Press, 1987.

Knightley, Philip, *The First Casualty: The War Correspondent as Hero, Propagandist and Myth Maker*, London, Quartet, 1982.
Kultgen, John, *Ethics and Professionalism*, Philadelphia, PA, University of Pennsylvania Press, 1988.
Lambeth, Edmund B., *Committed Journalism: An Ethic for the Profession*, Bloomington, Indiana University Press, 1986.
Lebacqz, Karen, *Professional Ethics: Power and Paradox*, Nashville, TN, Abingdon Press, 1985.
Lee, Simon, *The Cost of Free Speech*, London, Faber & Faber, 1990.
Leigh, David, *The Frontiers of Secrecy: Closed Government in Britain*, London, Junction Books, 1980.
Lichtenberg, Judith (ed.), *Democracy and the Mass Media*, Cambridge, Cambridge University Press, 1990.
MacNiven, Don (ed.), *Moral Expertise: Studies in Practical and Professional Ethics*, London, Routledge, 1989.
McQuail, Denis, *Media Performance: Mass Communications and the Public Interest*, London, Sage, 1992.
Malcolm, Janet, *The Journalist and the Murderer*, London, Bloomsbury, 1991.
Mercer, Derrik, Mungham, Geoff and Williams, Kevin, *The Fog of War: The Media on the Battlefield*, London, Heinemann, 1987.
Merrill, John C. (ed.), *The Dialectic in Journalism: Towards a Responsible Use of Press Freedom*, Baton Rouge, LA, Louisiana State University Press, 1989.
——*Global Journalism: A Survey of International Communication*, 2nd edn, New York, Longman, 1991.
Michael, James, *The Politics of Secrecy*, London, Penguin, 1982.
Morrison, David E. and Tumber, Howard, *Journalists at War: The Dynamics of News Reporting during the Falklands Conflict*, London, Sage, 1988.
Olen, Jeffrey, *Ethics in Journalism*, Englewood Cliffs, NJ, Prentice-Hall, 1988.
Paul, Noel S., *Principles for the Press: A Digest of Press Council Decisions, 1953–1984*, London, Press Council, 1985.
Pilger, John, *Heroes*, London, Jonathan Cape, 1986.
Pippert, Wesley G., *An Ethics of News: A Reporter's Search for Truth*, Washington DC, Georgetown University Press, 1989.
Ponting, Clive, *The Right to Know: The Inside Story of the Belgrano Affair*, London, Sphere, 1985.
—— *Secrecy in Britain*, Oxford, Blackwell, 1990.
Rivers, William L., Schramm, Wilbur and Christians, Clifford, *Responsibility in Mass Communication*, 3rd edn, New York, Harper & Row, 1980.
Robertson, Geoffrey, *Freedom, The Individual and the Law*, London, Penguin, 1989.
—— *People Against the Press: An Enquiry into the Press Council*, London, Quartet, 1983.
Rubin, Bernard, *Questioning Media Ethics*, New York, Praeger, 1978.
Schlesinger, Philip, *Media, State and Nation: Political Violence and Collective Identities*, London, Sage, 1991.

Schlesinger, Philip, Murdock, Graham and Elliott, Philip, *Televising 'Terrorism': Popular Violence in Popular Culture*, London, Comedia, 1983.
Schmuhl, Robert (ed.), *The Responsibilities of Journalists*, Notre Dame, IN, University of Notre Dame Press, 1984.
Schoeman, Ferdinand David (ed.), *Philosophical Dimensions of Privacy*, Cambridge: Cambridge University Press, 1984.
Seymour-Ure, Colin, *The British Press and Broadcasting Since 1945*, Oxford, Blackwell, 1991.
Sieghart, Paul, *The Lawful Rights of Mankind*, Oxford, Oxford University Press, 1985.
Turnbull, Malcolm, *The Spycatcher Trial*, London, Heinemann, 1988.
Wallace, Marjorie, *Campaign and Be Damned! The Place of Crusading Journalism – Past and Present – in a Secretive Society* (Second *Guardian* Lecture), Oxford, Nuffield College, 1991.
Wallington, Peter (ed.), *Civil Liberties 1984*, Oxford, Martin Robertson, 1984.
Whale, John, *The Politics of the Media*, 2nd edn, London, Fontana, 1980.
Whitehorn, Katharine, *Ethics and the Media*, Guildford, University of Surrey, 1988.
Wilson, Des (ed.), *The Secrets File: The Case for Freedom of Information in Britain Today*, London, Heinemann, 1984.
Wright, Peter, *Spycatcher: The Candid Autobiography of a Senior Intelligence Officer*, New York, Viking, 1987.

Index